KU-204-558

Contents

Introduction to

Ibiza
& Formentera

After decades of negative publicity that branded the island as little more than a budget ravers' paradise, Ibiza is rapidly reasserting itself as one of Spain's most cosmopolitan corners – an affluent, self-confident island with a fascinating heritage and a vibrant, home-grown music and fashion scene of global reach and importance.

▲ Santa Gertrudis

A pivotal part of the Carthaginian empire between 600 and 50 BC, Ibiza was closely linked with the fertility goddess Tanit and the god of dance Bes (from whom the name Ibiza is derived). Its status, however, declined under Roman occupation, and the island spent the next two thousand years as a backwater. Then, in the early 1960s, political opponents of Franco settled here and

▼ Ibiza Town's harbour

When to visit

Ibiza and Formentera are very warm between June and late September, when cloudless skies are virtually guaranteed. The heat can get intense in July and August, when highs in the 30s are common, but even at this time of year cooling sea breezes usually intervene to prevent things getting too uncomfortable. Winter in the Pitiuses is also glorious, with very little rainfall and temperatures normally high enough to enjoy sitting outside in cafés, even in January. As far as crowds go, there's a very clearly defined tourist season on both islands that begins slowly in early May, peaks in August when the islands get really packed, and slowly winds down throughout September. The last charter flights leave at the end of October. Winter is a wonderfully peaceful time for a visit, but flight connections are thin on the ground and there's little in the way of nightlife.

waves of beatniks discovered the island. Ibiza's decidedly bohemian character is rooted in this era, and remains particularly evident in the north of the island, where you'll find ethnic bazaars and hippy markets, as well as a large population of alternative types.

The island's natural beauty is captivating. Large swathes of the coastline survive in pristine condition, with sweeping sandy bays and exquisite coves tucked beneath soaring cliffs. Ibiza's hilly, thickly wooded interior is peppered with isolated whitewashed villages and ter-

◄ Atzaró agroturismo

raced fields of almonds, figs and olives. To really experience the scenic beauty and tranquility of the island's countryside, stay at an *agroturimo* (rural hotel) for a while; many excellent new places have opened in the last few years.

The charismatic capital, Ibiza Town, harbours most of the island's architectural treats, including a spectacular walled enclave, Dalt Vila, and a port area stuffed with hip bars, stylish restaurants and fashionable boutiques. Laying claim to be the

INTRODUCTION

Language

Catalan, not Castilian Spanish, is the official language of the islands, and we have therefore used Catalan names throughout the guide.

world's clubbing capital, Ibiza is an incredibly hedonistic place, where the nights are celebrated with unique spirit in landmark clubs scattered across the southern half of the island.

▲ Terrace, Amnesia

Serene, easy-going Formentera, the other main island of the Pitiuses (southern Balearics), is just a short ferry ride south of Ibiza yet offers a complete contrast. Boasting a relaxed, unhurried atmosphere and miles of ravishing sandy beaches lapped by translucent water, it has little or no nightlife and few historical sights apart from some sombre fortress churches and minor archeological ruins. It's the simplicity of life here, a back-to-nature appeal, that is Formentera's real allure.

▼ Santa Agnès coastal path, northwest Ibiza

Ibiza & Formentera
AT A GLANCE

IBIZA TOWN

Sassy Ibiza Town, the vibrant island capital, is one of the most scenic ports in the Mediterranean. The colossal medieval walls of its old *barrio*, Dalt Vila (a UNESCO World Heritage Site), provide a startlingly evocative backdrop and contain most of Ibiza's historic buildings, including the castle and cathedral.

▲ Harbour and Dalt Vila, Ibiza Town

SANT ANTONI

Offering enough bars in its West End zone to drown the devil himself, alongside the clubbing meccas of *Eden* and *Es Paradis* and the stylish lounge bars of the Sunset Strip, unpretentious Sant Antoni draws young clubbers in droves.

▼ Clubbing in Sant Antoni

▲ Harbour, Santa Eulària

SANTA EULÀRIA

This agreeable seaside town has an attractive marina and a historic hilltop quarter and there are several gorgeous cove beaches close by. Tuck into tapas on its famous street of restaurants, Carrer Sant Vicent.

▲ Countryside near Santa Agnès, northern Ibiza

NORTHERN IBIZA

Northern Ibiza is the least populated part of the island, its countryside a mix of pine-forested hills and rust-red terraced fields interspersed by diminutive villages. There's very little in the way of development to mar a coastline of isolated coves, rugged cliffs and lonely stone watchtowers – a hiker's delight.

SOUTHERN IBIZA

Endowed with over a dozen bite-shaped *calas* (coves), the shimmering Salines salt flats and the remarkable soaring offshore islet of Es Vedrà, southern Ibiza's coastline is extraordinarily beguiling.

▼ Cala Molí

FORMENTERA

The island of Formentera, comprising two flat promontories linked by a narrow sandy isthmus, is very thinly populated, much less developed than Ibiza and boasts stunning beaches surrounded by crystalline waters.

▼ Espalmador, Formentera

Ideas

The big six

Ibiza is rightly renowned for its nightlife, but the island also has a seductive beauty that begs exploration. Shaping up at just 50km by 18km, nowhere is more than an hour's drive away, while much smaller Formentera stretches only 15km from west to east. As well as almost innumerable cove beaches, the islands offer a fascinatingly diverse range of sights, from glistening bird-rich salt flats and soaring craggy cliffs to tranquil, architecturally historic villages.

▲ Ibiza Town

With a sublime harbour setting, a UNESCO World Heritage-listed medieval quarter, and a terrific choice of bars, restaurants and boutiques, Ibiza Town is unmissable.

P.51 ▸ IBIZA TOWN

▲ Salines saltpans

Both Ibiza and Formentera boast extensive salt flats, glittering pools of seawater first developed by the Phoenicians.

P.142 ▸ THE SOUTH
P.151 ▸ FORMENTERA

▲ Platja Illetes

The finest beach in the Balearics, this sublime slender finger of white sand lapped by shallow pellucid waters lies at Formentera's northern-most tip.

P.158 ▸ FORMENTERA

▶ Northern Ibiza

Ibiza's least populated and most rugged region, this is a bewitching land of thick pine forests, coastal cliffs and diminutive villages.

P.84 ▸ THE EAST
P.93 ▸ THE NORTHWEST

▼ Clubbing

House music's spiritual home, Ibiza serves up a selection of the globe's leading DJs virtually every night of the week in the summer months.

P.75 ▸ IBIZA TOWN
P.125 ▸ SANT ANTONI
P.146 ▸ THE SOUTH

▲ Es Vedrà

Looming above the southern coastline, this enigmatic 378-metre-high island looks magnificent from any angle.

P.135 ▸ THE SOUTH

Rural bliss

Nothing beats waking up to a view of fields of olive and almond trees stretching to pine-forested hills. Ibiza's rural hotel sector is booming, and there are plenty of terrific places to stay in all corners of the island. Most are converted farmhouses, extremely comfortable and stylishly decorated, and because the island is so small, it's easy to stay somewhere quite remote and still be close to the action.

▲ Atzaró

Setting new standards in the rural hotel sector, Atzaró has luxurious rooms, a spa, two pools and hosts a busy cultural program in summer.

P.104 ▶ THE NORTHWEST

▲ Can Talaias

This remote, relaxed country retreat boasts some of the best views in Ibiza from its position high on a hill above Cala Mastella.

P.89 ▶ THE EAST

▶ Can Pere

Classy and chic, this small, welcoming hotel has extensive grounds and enjoys sublime views of Ibiza's wooded hills.

`P.88 ▸ THE EAST`

▼ Can Martí

Close to the village of Sant Joan, this tranquil rustic place is set on a working organic farm, and run to strict environmental standards.

`P.104 ▸ THE NORTHWEST`

▲ Finca Can Xuxu

For an *agroturismo* experience that won't break the bank, check out this hip hotel close to the bays of Molí and Tarida.

`P.142 ▸ THE SOUTH`

Clubs

Ibiza is home to some of the planet's most celebrated club venues and the scene is potent enough to break new tunes and influence dance floors all over the world. A who's who of leading dance DJs play here in the summer season, when the atmosphere in the clubs can approach almost devotional intensity.

▲ Space

Now with twin terraces, myriad rooms and a huge balcony, Space is the best endowed club in Ibiza. Hosts a legendary 22-hour Sunday session.

P.147 › THE SOUTH

▲ Amnesia

Birthplace of the Balearic beat and the subsequent Acid house phenomenon, *Amnesia* today has some fearsome techno, progressive and trance nights.

P.125 › SANT ANTONI

◀ El Divino

A small, upmarket venue, *El Divino* concentrates on vocal house nights, and has a stunning harbourside setting.

P.76 ▸ IBIZA TOWN

▲ Pacha

More than just a club, Ibiza Town's *Pacha* is the base of an international dance empire, regularly hosting the world's leading turntablists. Offers a choice of different rooms and one of clubland's most elegant and enjoyable chillout terraces.

P.77 ▸ IBIZA TOWN

◀ Privilege

This venue – the biggest in the world – is quite extraordinary, housing a huge main arena complete with swimming pool, the *Coco Loco* (a club-within-a-club) and over a dozen bars.

P.128 ▸ SANT ANTONI

▶ DC10

Serving up pure mayhem every Monday, *DC10* draws Europe's party hardcore for a serious dancefloor mash-up.

P.146 ▸ THE SOUTH

Kids' Ibiza

Ibizans and Formenterans are extremely accommodating towards children, who are welcome in virtually all restaurants. With dozens of fine beaches and warm seas most of the year, children will be easily pleased. All of the family-oriented beaches have umbrellas and pedalos for hire, and most offer banana-boat trips for a speedy thrill.

▲ Go-karting

Test your boy-racer skills at one of Ibiza's two go-kart tracks, located on the Ibiza Town–Santa Eulària road and just outside Sant Antoni.

P.174 ▸ ESSENTIALS

▲ Beach fun

Pedal-powered floats are available for rent at every family-oriented beach in Ibiza, or for more of a thrill, ride the waves with an inflatable yellow fruit between your legs.

P.172 ▸ ESSENTIALS

▲ Aguamar

Waterworld extravaganza with a serpentine collection of chutes and slides, sure to bring a smile to the most jaded child (or adult).

P.140 ▶ THE SOUTH

▼ Tourist train

It doesn't run on rails, but a day out trundling through the Ibiza countryside on this contraption is sure to delight.

P.170 ▶ ESSENTIALS

Sunsets

Sunset watching is taken very seriously in Ibiza. Join the crowds at a stylish chillout bar where all chairs face west and you can sip a cocktail while taking in a blood-red Balearic sundown to a DJ's mix of emotive music. For something less commercialized, there are plenty of beautiful bays offering a more peaceful experience.

▲ Cala Saona

A terrific place in Formentera to catch the sun setting into the ocean, the craggy outlines of distant Ibiza and Es Vedrà defined against the pink horizon.

P.154 ▸ FORMENTERA

▲ Café Mambo

The crowds at its revamped terrace confirm that Café Mambo is one of the most hyped places on the planet to take in a sunset, but at least you're guaranteed a mighty DJ mix to match the scene.

P.124 ▸ SANT ANTONI

▲ Benirràs

Join the drummers and bong puffers at northern Ibiza's gorgeous cove beach to celebrate the spectacular Sunday sundown.

P.98 ▸ THE NORTHWEST

▼ Cala Salada

On winter days the islands opposite this bay create the perfect frame for a scarlet sunset.

P.117 ▸ SANT ANTONI

◀ Es Vedrà

Es Vedrà looks majestic at any time of day, but around sunset, purple and crimson hues give this island a hypnotic allure.

P.135 ▸ THE SOUTH

Shopping

Ibiza Town's port zone has dozens of zany boutiques selling everything from bargain-priced accessories to cutting-edge clubwear, with all the main designer labels well represented. Don't miss out on the quirky charm of Las Dalias if you're after anything with an ethnic flavour, and if you can't get that party anthem out of your head you'll find CD and vinyl specialists in Ibiza Town and Sant Antoni.

▼ El Secreto de Baltasar

Ibiza Town's most stylish shoe store, with hip footwear for men and women at affordable prices.

P.69 ▸ IBIZA TOWN

▼ Casi Todo auction house

From rustic farmhouse tables to rusty mountain bikes, this Santa Gertrudis auction house is a snooper's delight.

P.104 ▸ THE NORTHWEST

CASI TODO
Compra-Venta
Subastas
Tel. y Fax: 971197023
www.casitodo.com
SANTA GERTRUDIS

▲ Beachwear stalls

Many beaches – including Sa Caleta, Cala
d'Hort and Salines – have a market stall
or two selling a great selection of sarongs
and swimwear.

P.138, P.134 & P.141
▸ THE SOUTH

▶ Lotti Bogotti

Vintage store in Sant Carles with a wonderful
collection of jewellery made from hand-cut
stones and beads, plus cocktail dresses,
bags and accessories.

P.90 ▸ THE EAST

▼ Las Dalias market

All things Oriental – from Afghan rugs to
hubble-bubble pipes – in one of Ibiza's most
quirky markets.

P.92 ▸ THE EAST

Dine in style

From Asian fusion restaurants to wave-side seafood *chiringuitos* and rural retreats serving charcoal-grilled, island-reared meat, Ibiza hosts a real diversity of places to eat. Dalt Vila's pavement-terrace restaurants offer an evocative setting, but elsewhere many of the best places are off the beaten track – up a country lane or at the end of a potholed road. There's less choice on Formentera, but you'll find some great fish restaurants. Finish your meal with a shot of Hierbas liqueur or a Sa Caleta coffee.

▼ Bambuddha Grove

Asian restaurant-cum-lounge bar set in a gorgeous building of bamboo and thatch.

P.106 ▶ THE NORTHWEST

▼ Flipper & Chiller

The design of this place is a riot of day-glo oranges and pinks, but the nosh is very pukka, including fresh seafood and tempting salads.

P.164 ▶ THE FORMENTERA

◀ Es Boldado

Wonderful spot for paella, seafood or steak, high above Cala d'Hort with views across to Es Vedrà.

P.144 ▸ THE SOUTH

▲ Blue Marlin

A jet-set location on Cala Jondal beach, feast here from the modern, healthy menu then snooze it off on one of the posh sunbeds.

P.137 ▸ THE SOUTH

▼ La Paloma

Simply sublime village restaurant serving up imaginative, contemporary Mediterranean food based on seasonal local ingredients.

P.107 ▸ THE NORTHWEST

Port bars

Ibiza Town's riotous high-season port bar scene is founded on Spanish sociability, with added spice injected by the hordes of international party-goers that jet in each year. Grab a terrace seat for a ringside view of the theatrical club parades of costumed dancers that wind through the port's streets around midnight. The cavern-like bars on and around c/de la Verge have an underground, alternative feel and many of their owners are happy to advise on the best clubbing action and can often provide guest passes.

▲ Can Pou Bar

With moderate bar prices for the area, atmospheric *Can Pou* has a loyal (and mainly local) clientele, and is open all year.

P.73 ▶ IBIZA TOWN

▲ Bar Zuka

An intimate, stylish drinking den, this bar offers choice lounge and house music and is popular with club faces and Ibiza veterans.

P.72 ▶ IBIZA TOWN

▲ Rock Bar

With a huge harbourfront terrace and a
cosmopolitan vibe, this long-running venue
is an ideal place to enjoy Ibiza Town's unique
night scene.

P.73 ▶ IBIZA TOWN

▼ Noctámbula

Classic Sa Penya bar, run by a
party-geared Italian team, where
you're guaranteed a lively vibe and
accommodating service

P.73 ▶ IBIZA TOWN

Dalt Vila

A focal point for the whole island, its floodlit bastions and walls visible for miles around, Dalt Vila ("high town") is the hilltop above the capital, first settled by Phoenicians and now a UNESCO World Heritage site. Elegant and tranquil, most of its cobbled lanes are only passable by foot. Enter via the Portal de las Taules gateway and wind your way uphill, as all lanes lead to the cathedral-topped summit.

▼ Cathedral

Striking thirteenth-century Catalan Gothic structure with an impressive bell tower.

P.59 ▶ IBIZA TOWN

▲ Dining out

The many restaurant terraces make a historic setting for a memorable meal.

P.72 ▶ IBIZA TOWN

▶ Portal de ses Taules

An imposing Renaissance-era gateway, this is the grand main entrance into Dalt Vila.

P.55 ▶ IBIZA TOWN

▼ Museu Puget

This museum occupies a historic town house and has a comprehensive collection of local artist Narcís Puget's work.

P.58 ▶ IBIZA TOWN

MUSEU PUGET

Alternative Ibiza and Formentera

The islands' bohemian credentials are impeccable. It was already a haven for leftists opposed to Franco by the time American draft dodgers fleeing the call-up for the Korean and Vietnam wars flocked to the islands in the 1950s and 1960s. This countercultural tendency, including a liberal local attitude towards drug taking, sexuality, green issues and alternative thinking, endures.

▲ La Casita Verde

In an isolated spot north of Sant Josep, this ecological centre promotes sustainable living and welcomes volunteers (and visitors on Sundays).

P.139 ▶ THE SOUTH

▲ Punta de sa Galera

This small bay, also known as Cala Yoga, has flat rocky shelves ideal for sunbathing as well as more spiritual exercise.

P.116 ▶ SANT ANTONI

▲ Aigües Blanques

One of north Ibiza's finest beaches, popular with hippies and costume-free bathers.

P.86 ▸ THE NORTHWEST

▼ Hippodrome market

Ibiza's huge Saturday flea market is a great place to root around for vintage clothes and people-watch.

P.139 ▸ THE SOUTH

▶ Sa Penya boutiques

Kinky and kitsch, hip and happening, the boutiques on c/de la Verge stock what other stores don't or won't.

P.54 ▸ IBIZA TOWN

Formentera's beaches

It has been dubbed "the last Mediterranean paradise" by the tourist board – and for once the hyperbole is justified. Formentera's beautiful, sweeping sandy beaches are bordered by seas of exceptional clarity, and its tiny population and limited tourist development means that things never get too crowded here.

▲ s'Alga, Espalmador

Exquisite sheltered cove beach, with shallow, turquoise-tinged water.

P.159 ▶ FORMENTERA

▲ Es Pujols

Magnificent sandy stretch, relatively unaffected by the hotel infrastructure of the surrounding resort.

P.156 ▸ FORMENTERA

▲ Cala Saona

Fine cove beach with memorable sunset views from its fringes.

P.154 ▸ FORMENTERA

▲ Platja Illetes

A slender sandbar which stretches north towards Espalmador island, Formentera's finest beach is simply breathtaking from any angle.

P.158 ▸ FORMENTERA

▼ Platja de Migjorn

The longest beach in the southern Balearics, these sweeping sands are dotted with hip bars and restaurants.

P.160 ▸ FORMENTERA

Village churches

Ibiza and Formentera have an incredible collection of rural churches, with every village boasting a dazzling whitewashed place of worship. Simple, almost minimalist in form, their design (of Moorish origin) influenced Le Corbusier, the celebrated father of Modernist architecture. Most church interiors are stark and relatively unadorned – Republican troops angered by the Catholic Church's support for Franco torched most of their contents in the Civil War.

▼ Sant Carles

An archetypal Ibizan design, with white-washed walls and wonderfully simple lines.

P.84 ▶ THE EAST

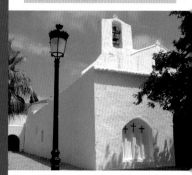

▼ Sant Miquel

Commanding a magnificent position above the village, the Església de Sant Miquel contains some elaborate frescoes.

P.98 ▶ THE NORTHWEST

▲ Santa Gertrudis

This eighteen-century church's broad facade (with stained glass windows) overlooks a crop of excellent village cafés.

P.103 ▸ FORMENTERA

▶ Jesús

The Nostra Mare de Jesús dates back to the fifteenth century, and has Ibiza's most impressive altar painting.

P.64 ▸ IBIZA TOWN

▼ Sant Jordi

An unexpected find in a mundane suburb, the unusual Església de Sant Jordi is topped with full battlements.

P.139 ▸ THE SOUTH

Deserted coves

Because Ibiza and Formentera are so thinly populated, with a combined population of around 130,000, it's easy to escape the crowds, even in July and August. To get to some of the finest cove beaches – bite-shaped pebble bays between soaring cliffs and sheltered sandy inlets – you'll need to negotiate rough dirt roads and hike along coastal paths.

▲ Sòl d'en Serra

Slender bay that's just a short walk from the resort of Cala Llonga, with a bar-restaurant above its pebble beach.

P.78 ▸ THE EAST

▼ Platja Codolar

Impressive expanse of wave-polished stones and barely a soul in sight.

P.139 ▸ THE SOUTH

▲ Cala d'en Serra

Barely a niche in the coastline, this little beach has a good *chiringuito* for drinks and meals.

P.97 ▶ THE NORTHWEST

▼ s'Estanyol

Attractive little sandy cove beach, close to Ibiza Town, with great food available in the shoreside *chiringuito*.

P.64 ▶ IBIZA TOWN

▼ Portitxol

A startling horseshoe-shaped cove on Ibiza's most remote coastline.

P.100 ▶ NORTHWEST

Gay Ibiza

Ibiza has been one of Europe's main gay destinations since the 1960s, although the lesbian scene is very limited. Ibiza Town has a gay quarter with bars, a club, and dozens of stores and restaurants and the island also offers a stunning beach that is popular with gay men. Most gay visitors stay in either Ibiza Town or Figueretes.

▲ La Troya Asesina

Perhaps the best gay club night in Spain, held at *Space* and simply not to be missed.

P.147 ▶ THE SOUTH

▲ Carrer de la Verge

The heart of Ibiza's gay village, a historic portside street full of gay-owned businesses and bars.

P.54 ▶ IBIZA TOWN

▲ Es Cavallet beach

Es Cavallet is arguably the finest beach in southern Ibiza, and its gay zone has the best stretch of sand, as well as the wonderful *Chiringay* restaurant.

P.141 ▸ THE SOUTH

▼ Dôme

The *grande dame* of the gay bar scene – head here to catch the club parades around 1am.

P.74 ▸ IBIZA TOWN

Hippy heritage

In the 1960s and 1970s, Ibiza and Formentera were one of Europe's key hippy destinations, drawing bohemian folk from all over the world, including musicians Pink Floyd (who recorded in Formentera), Bob Dylan and King Crimson. Relations between the "hairies" and locals were generally good, but there were regular bust-ups with the Guardia Civil over drug use and nudity. Many hippies never left the island, settling in the north of Ibiza around Sant Joan and in La Mola in Formentera.

▼ Atlantis

Near-mythical cove, housing an ancient quarry whose rock face has been carved with cosmic imagery.

P.136 ▸ THE SOUTH

▼ Yoga retreats

The practice of yoga has been popular in Ibiza since the 1960s, and the island has plenty of options for yogis.

P.175 ▸ ESSENTIALS

▲ Las Dalias

This famous bar-restaurant in Sant Carles hosts psy-trance, world music and Indian-themed nights and a boho Saturday market.

P.84 ▸ THE EAST

▲ Benirràs beach

Ibiza hippydom's favourite beach – many folk gather here around sunset near the small *chiringuito* at the far end of the bay.

P.98 ▸ THE NORTHWEST

◀ Formentera's windmills

Bob Dylan is said to have lived in a windmill outside La Mola, while the Pink Floyd album *More* features another on its cover.

P.162 ▸ FORMENTERA

Hiking

Ibiza and Formentera are terrific places to explore by foot, with some beautiful country trails that pass fields of wildflowers and diminutive villages. It's the coastal hikes, however, that really stand out, offering wonderful views over the Mediterranean. Low annual rainfall and mild, sunny winters mean walking is an option year-round and superb outside the main tourist season.

▲ South of Platja d'en Bossa

Lovely hike on a thickly wooded coastal path, leading to the southernmost point in Ibiza.

P.140 ▶ THE SOUTH

▼ Around Santa Agnès

One of Ibiza's most scenic sections of coastline, this path runs past steep cliffs and through terraced fields that have been reclaimed by pine forests.

P.102 ▶ THE NORTHWEST

▲ Up Sa Talaiassa

The steep hour or so's ascent from the village of Sant Josep to Ibiza's highest peak offers panoramic views of the island.

P.131 ▸ THE SOUTH

▼ To Atlantis

From the watchtower of Torre des Savinar it's a terrific, if steep, hike down to the old coastal quarry known as Atlantis.

P.136 ▸ THE SOUTH

Off the beaten track

Armed with a map, it's surprisingly easy to really escape the crowds in Ibiza and Formentera, and there are some wild and pristine landscapes to enjoy. Staking the coast like sentinels are a chain of barely visited stone watchtowers that would have been manned night and day in centuries past, while isolated bays such as the magnificent Cala d'Aubarca are rarely visited by anyone.

▲ Estany des Peix

The rocky land around the western fringes of Formentera's "lake of fish" has a desolate beauty.

P.152 ▸ FORMENTERA

▲ Cala d'Aubarca

The descent to one of the wildest, most remote corners of Ibiza has to be done on foot.

P.101 ▸ THE NORTHWEST

▲ Cap de Barbària

Windswept and bleak, Formentera's Barbària peninsula is at its most stirring around its southern tip.

P.155 ▶ FORMENTERA

▼ Torre des Savinar

High in the southern coastal cliffs opposite Es Vedrà, this is the most evocatively situated of all the islands' old stone defence towers

P.135 ▶ THE SOUTH

44

Historic Ibiza

Ibiza and Formentera may not offer world-class historical sights, but there are plenty of curious buildings and places of interest, including a vast necropolis, cave shrines and fortified churches.

▲ Puig des Molins

Explore the tombs of this 4000-year-old Punic necropolis, situated in the heart of Ibiza Town.

P.61 ▸ IBIZA TOWN

▲ Puig de Misa

The historic heart of Santa Eulària, this hilltop houses a church that dates back to the thirteenth century and an ethnographic museum.

P.82 ▶ THE EAST

▼ Església de Sant Antoni

Once topped with cannons, Sant Antoni's fine fortified church is hidden in the backstreets of town.

P.112 ▶ SANT ANTONI

▲ Dalt Vila's walls

These mighty, forebidding walls were never breached by pirates, and have survived in perfect condition.

P.54 ▶ IBIZA TOWN

Watersports

Ibiza and Formentera are perfect for watersports, with clean seas and dozens of experienced centres offering quality tuition and equipment. Some of the best locations for diving and sailing are around the offshore islets at places like Conillera and Tagomago, well away from the main tourist resorts.

▲ Windsurfing

Most of the resorts have windsurfing schools where you can hire gear, and there are challenging breezes for most of the year.

P.173 ▶ ESSENTIALS

▲ Scuba diving and snorkelling

With exceptional visibility and plenty of fascinating marine life, Ibiza and Formentera offer superb diving and snorkelling.

P.172 ▸ ESSENTIALS

▼ Fishing and catamaran trips

Whether you want to dangle a line or mimic Duran Duran on the ocean wave, chartered boat trips are easy to set up.

P.173 ▸ ESSENTIALS

▲ Sailing

Conditions are usually excellent, and there are a dozen schools where you can learn to sail, or improve your skills.

P.173 ▸ ESSENTIALS

Places

Ibiza Town and around

Urbane Ibiza Town (Eivissa) is the cultural and administrative heart of the island. Set around a dazzling natural harbour, it's one of the Mediterranean's most charismatic pocket-sized capitals, full of hip boutiques and chic bars and restaurants. In the summer months, its narrow whitewashed lanes become an alfresco catwalk, as a good selection of the planet's fashionistas and party freaks strut the streets in an orgy of competitive hedonism. Looming above the port is historic Dalt Vila, a rocky escarpment topped by a walled enclave, squabbled over by the island's invaders since the days of the Phoenicians. The fortress-like Catalan cathedral and craggy Moorish castle that bestride the summit are Ibiza's most famous landmarks, visible across much of the south of the island. Below Dalt Vila, Ibiza Town's harbour is the island's busiest, its azure waters ruffled by a succession of yachts, container ships and ferries. To the west is the New Town, only really attractive in the streets close to boulevard-like Vara de Rey, while, occupying the north side of the bay, the New Harbour zone is an upmarket pleasure strip. Around Ibiza Town, you'll find a couple of beaches of varying quality and some good café-bars in the village of Jesús.

PLACES

Ibiza Town and around

Arrival and information

A new **bus station** is due to open in mid-2008, just off the Can Misses roundabout, opposite the Multicines complex (see map, p.52–53). This is about 1.5km west of the port area, though regular services will connect the new terminal with the town centre.

Until it opens, all buses depart from outside the small, scruffy ticket office on Avgda d'Isidor Macabich. Buses run to/from the airport (May–Oct every 30min until 11.30pm; Nov–April hourly until 10pm). Routes and times to all other destinations are included in the relevant entries in the text; you can also consult ⊛www .ibizabus.com. **Boats** (all May–Oct only) dock on the south side of the harbour for a number of destinations including Talamanca, Platja d'en Bossa and Santa Eulària. All boats to Formentera leave from a terminal on Avgda Santa Eulària, on the west side of the harbour.

Ibiza Town's efficient **tourist information** office is located opposite the Estació Marítima (port building) on the Passeig Marítim harbourfront (June–Sept Mon–Fri 9am–1.30pm & 5–7pm, Sat 10.30am–1pm; Oct–May Mon–Fri 8.30am–2.30pm; ☏971 301 900).

and the walls of Dalt Vila in the south. Its alleys and tiny plazas are crammed with fashionable stores, restaurants and bars, and the almost souk-like streets fizz with life until the early hours during high season. By the end of September, however, the pace abates, most of the restaurants and bars shut up shop, and the area becomes a virtual ghost town.

Along Passeig Marítim

The best place to start exploring La Marina is at the southwestern corner of the harbourfront, along Passeig Marítim. Heading east, a cluster of upmarket café-bars (try *Mar y Sol*) afford fine vistas of the yachts and docks. Past the midway point, marked by the modern harbour building, the Estació Marítima, the street is lined with restaurants and bars.

▲ LA MARINA

La Marina

La Marina, Ibiza Town's atmospheric harbourside district, often just referred to as *el puerto* ("the port"), is the heart of the Ibizan capital. A crooked warren of narrow streets, it's sandwiched between the harbour waters to the north

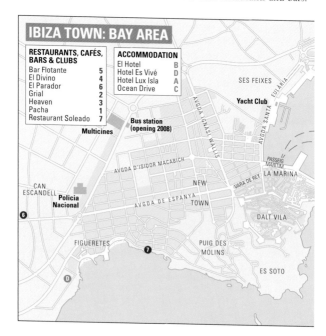

IBIZA TOWN: BAY AREA

RESTAURANTS, CAFÉS, BARS & CLUBS
Bar Flotante 5
El Divino 4
El Parador 6
Grial 2
Heaven 3
Pacha 1
Restaurant Soleado 7

ACCOMMODATION
El Hotel B
Hotel Es Vivé D
Hotel Lux Isla A
Ocean Drive C

▲ CLUB PARADE

These venues provide an ideal standpoint for taking in the outrageous club parades that are such a feature of the Ibizan night in high season, featuring processions of costumed dancers and drag queens bearing banners that promote events at the big club venues. Further along, the tiny **Plaça de sa Riba**, backed by tottering old whitewashed fishermen's houses, makes an agreeable place for outdoor dining. At the very end of the *passeig*, the breakwater of Es Muro extends into the harbour, offering an excellent view back over the old town, and a flight of steps heads south up into Sa Penya (see p.54).

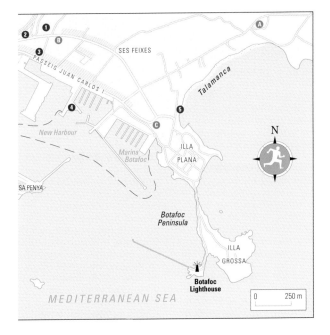

Dalt Vila's walls

Encircling the entire historic quarter of Dalt Vila, Ibiza Town's monumental Renaissance-era **walls** are the city's most distinctive structure. Completed in 1585 and still in near-perfect condition, the walls – at almost 2km long, 25m high and up to 5m thick – are some of Europe's best-preserved fortifications, and form a key part of the city's UNESCO World Heritage recognition. The Carthaginians built walls close to today's castle around the fifth century BC, and these were extended during the Moorish occupation – remnants from this period can be seen inside La Curia (see p.59) on c/Mayor. Battered by centuries of attacks from pirates, the city's crumbling walls were replaced in the sixteenth century by vast new fortifications, designed by Giovanni Battista Calvi and Jacobo Fratín, that included seven colossal bastions (*baluards*).

Església de Sant Elm

Open only for mass. The Església de Sant Elm, burnt down at least a dozen times by pirates, was first built in the fifteenth century. A sturdy, functional three-storey design with a tiered bell-tower, the present building was constructed after the last church was destroyed during the Spanish Civil War. The cool interior is home to the shell of a giant clam (which doubles as the church font) and a striking statue of a beaming open-armed Christ, complete with 1960s-style hairdo. The other image of interest is the haloed *Verge del Carmen* (Carmen the Virgin), carrying a child, which has long been associated with the Ibizan seamen's guild and the July 16 fiesta (see p.176).

Plaça de sa Constitució

This small, peaceful square of elegant whitewashed and ochre-painted old merchants' houses is home to Es Mercat Vell ("The Old Market"), a curiously squat Neoclassical edifice where fruit and vegetables have been traded since 1873 – today the stalls specialize in organic produce. The square is a great place for a refuelling stop before the steep assault on Dalt Vila – try the ever-popular, if chaotic *Croissant Show* (see p.69).

Sa Penya

Sa Penya, a twisted triangle of streets hemmed in by the city walls to the south and the sea to the north, is both Ibiza's gay village and its main gypsy district, home to one of the most marginalized of Spain's communities. Its crumbling facades, dark, warren-like alleys and lanes and outrageous streetlife, bars and boutiques are home to an edgy, vibrant and absorbing scene. If you want to explore the *barrio* it's probably best to stick to the area around Carrer d'Alfons XII and Carrer de la Verge, as the quieter streets are poorly lit and can be unsafe at night.

Carrer de la Verge

Cutting through the heart of Sa Penya, Carrer de la Verge (also signposted as Carrer de la Mare de Déu) is *the* gay street in Ibiza, lined with dozens of tiny cave-like bars and restaurants, plus a fetish boutique or two. Despite its inappropriate moniker, the "Street of the Virgin" is easily the wildest on the island. An ordinary-looking, sleepy lane by day, at night it metamorphoses into a dark, urban alley dedicated to gay hedonism, reverberating to pounding hard house and all-round cacophony. Moving west to east, the street becomes progressively busier, narrower and more raucous, finally becoming no more than a couple of paces wide and crammed with perfectly honed muscle (and a dodgy 'tache or two). Up on the balconies, drag queens and club dancers preen themselves for the long night ahead, while down below a frenzy of flirtation and bravado fills the air. Just before the rocky cliff that signifies the end of the street, **Sa Torre**, a small defensive tower, is a wonderful place to take in night-time views of the lights of Formentera and the Botafoc peninsula.

Carrer d'Alfons XII

During daylight hours Carrer d'Alfons XII is a pleasant but unremarkable corner of Sa Penya, framed by five- and six-storey whitewashed houses and the city walls. Dotted with palm-shaded benches, it's bordered by a small octagonal building, the city's old **fish market**, which rarely opens these days. By night, however, the plaza-like street is transformed into one of Ibiza's most flamboyant arenas – the final destination for the summer club parades. At around 1am, after an hour or so of posturing, the podium dancers, promoters and drag queens come together here for a final encore, which sees a surging, sociable throng spill out of some of the most stylish bars on the island to people-watch, blag guest passes and discuss plans for the night's clubbing.

Portal de ses Taules

The main entrance into Dalt Vila is the appropriately imposing Portal de ses Taules ("Gate of the Inscriptions"). The approach alone quickens the pulse: up a mighty stone ramp, across a drawbridge and over a dried-up moat – all part of the defences necessary to keep out sixteenth-century pirates. A stone plaque mounted above the gate bears the coat of arms of Felipe II. Flanking the *portal* are two white marble statues (replicas of a Roman soldier and the goddess Juno). After passing through the gateway, you enter the old **Pati d'Armes** (armoury court), a surprisingly graceful, shady arena – the island's very first hippy market was held here in the 1960s. The armoury court leads into graceful **Plaça de Vila**, bordered by elegant old whitewashed mansions, where there are pavement cafés, upmarket restaurants and an

▼ PORTAL DE SES TAULES

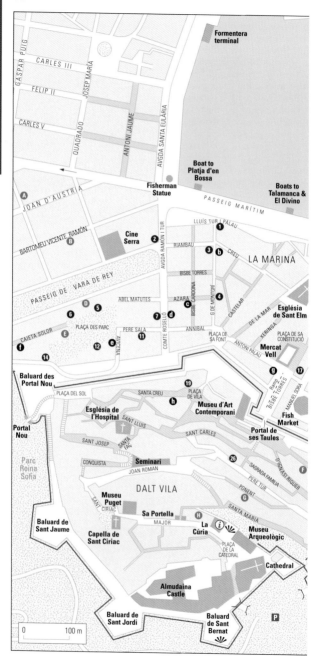

Formentera terminal

Boat to Platja d'en Bossa

Boats to Talamanca & El Divino

Fisherman Statue

PASSEIG MARÍTIM

LLUÍS TUR I PALAU 1

RIAMBAU 3 b CREU

LA MARINA

GASPAR PUIG

CARLES III

JOSEP MARÍA

FELIP II

CARLES V

QUADRADO

ANTONI JAUME

AVGDA SANTA EULÀRIA

JOAN D'AUSTRIA A

BARTOMEU VICENTE RAMÓN B

Cine Serra 2

AVGDA RAMON I TUR

PASSEIG DE VARA DE REY

ABEL MATUTES

BISBE TORRES

AZARA C

BISBE CARDONA

G DE MONTGRÍ

CASTELAR

DE LA MAR

Església de Sant Elm

6 5

D 0

CAIETA SOLOR E

PLAÇA DES PARC

12

AVICENNA

COMTE ROSELLÓ

PERE SALA

7 d

11

ANNIBAL

PLAÇA DE SA FONT

ANTONI PALAU

XERINGA

PLAÇA DE SA CONSTITUCIÓ

Mercat Vell

9

17

f

14

Baluard des Portal Nou

PLAÇA DEL SOL

SANTA CREU

PLAÇA DE VILA 19

h

Museu d'Art Contemporani

Ramp

BISBE TORRES

MANUEL SORÀ

Fish Market

Portal Nou

Església de l'Hospital

SANT LLUÍS

SANT CARLES

Portal de ses Taules

SANT JOSEP

SANTA FAV

Parc Reina Sofia

CONQUISTA

JOAN ROMAN

Seminari

26

SAGRADA FAMILIA

D'ABAST RIQUER

F

DALT VILA

PERE TUR

PONENT

G

Museu Puget

SANT CIRIAC

Sa Portella

MAJOR

La Cúria

SANTA MARIA

i

Museu Arqueològic

Capella de Sant Ciriac

H

PLAÇA DE LA CATEDRAL

Cathedral

Baluard de Sant Jaume

Almudaina Castle

P

Baluard de Sant Jordi

Baluard de Sant Bernat

0   100 m

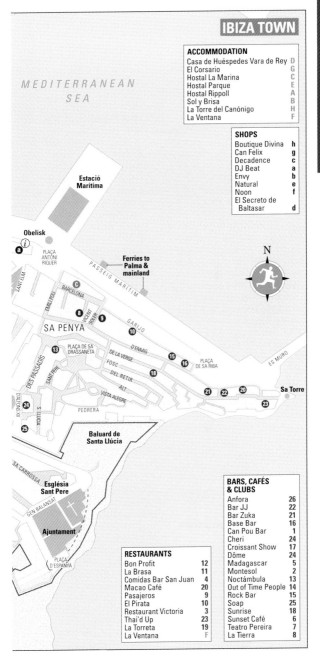

IBIZA TOWN

ACCOMMODATION

Casa de Huéspedes Vara de Rey	D
El Corsario	G
Hostal La Marina	C
Hostal Parque	E
Hostal Rippoll	A
Sol y Brisa	B
La Torre del Canónigo	H
La Ventana	F

SHOPS

Boutique Divina	h
Can Felix	g
Decadence	c
DJ Beat	a
Envy	b
Natural	e
Noon	f
El Secreto de Baltasar	d

MEDITERRANEAN SEA

Estació Marítima

Obelisk

PLAÇA ANTÒNI RIQUER

PASSEIG MARÍTIM

Ferries to Palma & mainland

N

BARCELONA

VICENT SERR

SA PENYA

GARIJO

D'ENMIG

PLAÇA DE SA DRASSANETA

DE LA VERGE

FOSC

PLAÇA DE SA RIBA

DEL RETIR

ES MURO

ALT

VISTA ALEGRE

Sa Torre

PEDRERA

DES PASSADÍS

SANT PERE

SANT ELM

EMAU IPOU

D'ALGNS XII

STA LLÚCIA

Baluard de Santa Llúcia

SA CARROSSA

Església Sant Pere

GEN BALANSAT

Ajuntament

PLAÇA D'ESPANYA

RESTAURANTS

Bon Profit	12
La Brasa	11
Comidas Bar San Juan	4
Macao Café	20
Pasajeros	9
El Pirata	10
Restaurant Victoria	3
Thai'd Up	23
La Torreta	19
La Ventana	F

BARS, CAFÉS & CLUBS

Anfora	26
Bar JJ	22
Bar Zuka	21
Base Bar	16
Can Pou Bar	1
Cheri	24
Croissant Show	17
Dôme	24
Madagascar	5
Montesol	2
Noctámbula	13
Out of Time People	14
Rock Bar	15
Soap	25
Sunrise	18
Sunset Café	6
Teatro Pereira	7
La Tierra	8

assortment of art galleries and boutiques.

Dalt Vila

Occupying a craggy peak south of the harbour, the ancient settlement of Dalt Vila ("High Town") is the oldest part of Ibiza Town and one of its quietest corners. The inhabitants are a disparate mix: the clergy, pockets of Ibizan high society, gypsy families and foreigners seduced by the superb views and tranquil atmosphere. Alongside the major attractions there are a number of sights to look out for including the walls themselves (see box on p.54), and the unadorned whitewashed facade of the fifteenth-century **Església de l'Hospital** – once a hospital for the poor, now a low-key cultural centre – at the end of Carrer Sant Josep. **Carrer Major** contains some of the grandest mansions (some bearing family coats-of-arms), the new Museu Puget (see below), and, close to its western end, a curious chapel, the **Capella de Sant Ciriac**. Little more than a shrine in the wall protected by a metal grille, it is said to be the entrance to a secret tunnel through which the Catalans and Aragonese stormed the Moorish citadel on August 8, 1235 – a special mass is held here to mark the date (see p.176).

Museu d'Art Contemporani

Closed for renovation until 2010. Ibiza's Museu d'Art Contemporani is housed in a former arsenal; the building was begun in 1727 and later used as a barracks and as the stables of the Infantry Guard. As the premises are currently being expanded, with plans to occupy an additional building, the museum will be closed until 2010. When it reopens, check out the work of island-born Tur Costa and the challenging abstract art of Ibiza visitors Will Faber, Hans Hinterreiter and Erwin Broner.

Museu Puget

c/Major. May–Sept Tues–Fri 10am–1.30pm & 5–8pm, Sat & Sun 10am–1.30pm; Oct–April Tues–Fri 10am–1.30pm & 4–6pm, Sat & Sun 10am–1.30pm. Free. This new museum has a large permanent collection of paintings and photographs by renowned Ibizan artist Narcís Puget Viñas (1874–1960), including some superb monochrome images of the island. The museum building, which dates back to the fifteenth century, is also of considerable interest and was once one of Ibiza's grandest mansions. Known as Can Comasema, it boasts a fine facade with Gothic-style windows, a delightful central courtyard, and wonderful views of the harbour.

Museu Arqueològic d'Eivissa i Formentera

Plaça de la Catedral. April–Sept Tues–Sat 10am–2pm & 5–7.30pm, Sun 10am–2pm; Oct–March Tues–Sat 10am–1pm & 4–6pm, Sun 10am–2pm. €2.50. The Museu Arqueològic d'Eivissa i Formentera provides an overview of Pitiusan history from prehistoric times to the end of Islamic rule in the thirteenth century. It's not wildly exciting, but the exhibits are logically arranged and well presented. The building itself is also of interest, its simple stone facade belying a much bigger interior and its role as the Universitat, Ibiza's seat of government until 1717. There's a fine, ribbed vault roof in the museum's entrance hall (originally a chapel) that dates from the fourteenth century.

Modest prehistoric and Phoenician remains are housed in the first two rooms, while the Carthaginian exhibits are also pretty meagre considering Ibiza's importance at that time. There is, however, a carved limestone *stela*, with an inscription dedicated to the fearsome god Baal, who was associated with a cult involving the sacrifice of children, plus earthenware images of the fertility goddess Tanit. Aside from the original statues the copies mounted by the Portal de ses Taules (see p.55) were based on, there's an interesting Roman coin or two with the image of the Carthaginian god Bes on the reverse side, reflecting the fairly harmonious crossover between Punic and Roman times.

Cathedral

Daily June–Nov 9.30am–1.30pm & 4–7pm, Dec–May 9.30am–1.30pm & 6–9pm; services take place on Sun at 10.30am. Free. Dalt Vila's strategic importance is obvious once you reach Plaça de la Catedral, which affords magnificent views over the port area to the open ocean and Formentera. This summit has been a place of worship for two and a half millennia, and the site for a succession of ceremonial structures: Carthaginian and Roman temples, a Moorish-built mosque and the Gothic Catalan cathedral that stands here today. A former parish church, it was granted cathedral status in 1782 and dedicated to Santa Maria de les Neus (Mary of the Snows).

Built mostly in the mid-fourteenth century, the cathedral is a simple rectangular

▲ CATHEDRAL

structure supported by buttresses and topped by a mighty bell-tower. Its sombre, uncluttered lines are at their most aesthetically pleasing from a distance, especially from across the harbour at night, when the structure is floodlit. Whitewashed throughout, the interior is much less attractive, with somewhat trite Baroque embellishments. Close to the entrance door there's a plaque dedicated to the Francoists and Catholics massacred in 1936 by Catalan Anarchists (see p.182).

The cathedral also contains the **Museu Diocesà** (same hours but closed Sun; €1.50), which is dedicated to religious art, and takes in a brooding collection of religious portraits and the odd ecclesiastical curio, including some Renaissance choirbooks.

La Cúria

Across from the cathedral is **La Cúria**, a late Gothic-style courthouse that now contains a tourist information desk (Tues–Sun 10am–2pm &

5–8pm) and an impressive new **interpretive centre** (Tues–Fri 10am–1.30pm & 5–8pm, Sat & Sun 10am–1.30pm; free), dedicated mainly to Ibiza's Muslim era, when the island was known as Yebisah. Excavated sections of medieval defensive walls are laid bare, and there are exhibits of Moorish pottery, Qu'rans and high-tech displays that offer computer-generated images and videos of life in Islamic Ibiza.

The castle

A rambling strip of buildings constructed in a fractious contest of architectural styles, the castle squats atop the very highest ground in Dalt Vila. Construction began in the eighth century, although modifications were still being made as late as the eighteenth century. During the Spanish Civil War, the castle was the setting for one of the darkest chapters in Ibizan history, when mainland Anarchists, briefly in control of the island, massacred over a hundred Ibizan Nationalist prisoners before

fleeing the island. A lengthy renovation is now ongoing that will transform the near-derelict remains of the castle into one of Spain's state-owned Parador hotels, though it's unlikely to open before 2011 at the earliest.

For the best perspective of the crumbling facade, head south to the Baluard de Sant Bernat. From here you can make out the sixteenth-century former governor's residence – slab-fronted, dusty pink and with three iron balconies – and rising above this to the left the towers of the Almudaina, the Moorish keep. Smack in the middle of the castle complex is a Moorish fortification, the Tower of Homage, while dropping down to the left are the wonky-windowed eighteenth-century infantry barracks.

The southerly views from Sant Bernat are also spectacular, with Formentera clearly visible on the horizon and the sprawling Ibizan resorts of Figueretes and Platja d'en Bossa hugging the coastline just a couple of kilometres away.

Plaça d'Espanya and Sa Carrossa

Directly below the cathedral, Plaça d'Espanya is a narrow, open-ended cobbled square shaded by palm trees. The imposing arcaded building with the domed roof that dominates the plaza was originally built as a Dominican monastery in 1587, before being converted to today's **Ajuntament** (town hall). To the rear of the Ajuntament is one of Ibiza's most handsome churches, the whitewashed sixteenth-century **Església de Sant Pere** (also known as Sant Domingo, and open only for services), topped by red-tiled domes and

▼ ISIDOR MACABICH

▲ BUSKERS, PLAÇA DES PARC

constructed by Genoese master craftsmen. At the eastern end of the plaza (from where there are fine sea views) is a recumbent statue of Guillem de Montgrí, a crusading Catalan baron who helped drive the Moors from Ibiza in 1235. It's a short walk from here along the edge of the walls to the vast, five-sided **Baluard de Santa Llúcia**, the largest of the seven bastions that define the perimeters of Ibiza Town's walls; rows of cannons are mounted along its battlements.

West of here, pretty **Sa Carrossa**, lined with restaurants, plane trees and flowering shrubs, has a statue of a miserable-looking figure: historian and Ibizan author Isidor Macabich, though he was known for his sardonic sense of humour.

Vara de Rey and around

An imposing and graceful tree-lined boulevard with beautiful early twentieth-century buildings, Vara de Rey is the hub of modern Ibiza. It's here that you'll find the island's oldest cinema, the Art Deco-style Cine Serra, one of Ibiza's most famous café-bars, the *Montesol* (see p.73), and a collection of fashionable boutiques. Smack in the middle of the avenue is a large

stone-and-iron monument dedicated to Ibiza-born General Joachim Vara de Rey, who died in the Battle of Caney fought between Spain and the USA over Cuba in 1889.

Just a block to the south, the **Plaça des Parc** is an even more inviting place for a coffee or a snack, night or day, with a myriad of café-bars and restaurants grouped around a square shaded by acacias and palms. There's no traffic at all to contend with here, and the small plaza attracts an intriguing mix of stylish Ibizan denizens and bohemian characters. The bars all have plenty of atmosphere: try *Sunset Café* or *Madagascar* (see p.69).

Puig des Molins

Necropolis: March–Oct Tues–Sat 10am–2pm & 6–8pm, Sun 10am–2pm; Nov–Feb Tues–Sat 9am–3pm, Sun 10am–2pm. Free. Five minutes' walk south of Vara de Rey, Puig des Molins ("Hill of the Windmills") was one of the most important Punic burial sites in the Mediterranean. It was chosen by the Phoenicians in the seventh century BC because their burial requirements specified a site free from poisonous creatures – there are no snakes or scorpions on Ibiza. Noblemen

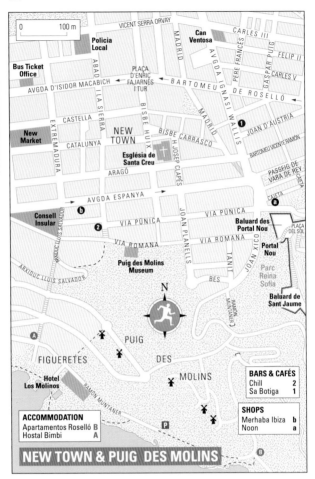

NEW TOWN & PUIG DES MOLINS

were buried on this necropolis in their thousands, their bodies transported here from all over the empire.

Despite its UNESCO World Heritage status, Puig des Molins today is pretty unassuming to look at, appearing little more than a barren rocky park scattered with olive trees. However, the hillside is riddled with over three thousand tombs, and excavations over the years

have unearthed some splendid terracotta figurines, amphorae and amulets; most of the finds are gathered in the museum building adjacent to the site, which has been closed for years, but should reopen by 2010. A short trail winds around the site, passing Chamber 3, which contains thirteen stone sarcophagi from Punic times. There are also some Punic artefacts at the Museu

Arqueològic d'Eivissa i Formentera (see p.58).

New Harbour and Botafoc

Occupying the western and northern sides of Ibiza Town's bay, the New Harbour (or "Port d'Eivissa") is a recent extension to the city. This area was one half of the capital's vegetable patch, Ses Feixes, until the late 1950s, when the town began to expand to the north. Today, it's a wealthy enclave containing the yacht club, several marinas, luxury apartment blocks, the casino and the clubs *El Divino, Heaven* and *Pacha* (see p.76 & p.77).

From the *Ocean Drive* hotel, the slender, kilometre-long Botafoc peninsula stretches southeast into the harbour, with a wide road running along its length and a lighthouse defining its final rocky extremity – cava-swigging revellers traditionally congregate here to witness the first sunrise of the New Year. Beyond the lighthouse, a new concrete dock juts into the harbour waters, offering photographers an arresting perspective of the fortress-like summit of Dalt Vila across the waves.

Talamanca

Boat from La Marina, May–Oct 9am–1am every 15–30min; 10min. A sweeping sandy bay 2km north of Ibiza Town (a 30min walk via the New Harbour along Passeig de Juan Carlos I), Talamanca Beach rarely gets overcrowded, despite its close proximity to the capital. New building has been fairly restrained here, with hotels mainly confined to the northern and southern fringes, and it's not impossible to imagine the natural beauty of the beach before it was developed for tourism. A smattering of bars and some good fish restaurants occupy the central part of the shoreline, which is popular with European families – the gently shelving beach is ideal for children.

Just behind the northern section of the beach, the

▼ BOTAFOC LIGHTHOUSE

▲ TALAMANCA BEACH

upmarket suburb of **Can Pep Simó** contains a cluster of striking Modernist villas designed by the Catalan architect Josep Lluís Sert.

s'Estanyol

Best approached from the north side of Talamanca Beach, on a signposted route that takes you 1km or so down a tarmacked road, then 2km down a bumpy dirt track, the idyllic sandy cove of s'Estanyol is one of Ibiza's most isolated bays. There's a small patch of sand and plenty of rocky ledges for sunbathing, as well as one of the island's best *chiringuitos* (beach café-bars), the funky *PK s'Estanyol* (daily May–Oct and some sunny winter days), selling fresh fish and paella feasts for around €25 a head. This *chiringuito* is also occasionally used as an after-party venue.

Jesús

Just northeast of Ibiza Town, along the road to Cala Llonga, Jesús is an overspill of the capital suspended in a suburban no-man's land; it's just urban enough to boast a fine café (*Croissantería Jesús*, see p.69), but rural enough to ensure that

roosters prevent any chance of a lie-in.

Just off the highway in the centre of the village, the **Nostra Mare de Jesús** (Thurs 10am–noon, plus Sunday Mass) boasts a wonderfully simple Ibizan design, with an unadorned whitewashed facade, that dates back to 1466. The church has the island's finest altar painting by Valencians, Pere de Cabanes and Rodrigo de Osona. An impressive and expansive work spread over seven main and thirteen smaller panels, with images of Christ, the Virgin Mary and the Apostles, it was deemed of sufficient artistic merit to be spared during the Civil War, when most of the island's religious art was destroyed. Opposite the church is the lively bar *Bon Lloc* (see p.70).

Figueretes

The suburb-cum-resort of Figueretes lies only a fifteen-minute walk southwest of the capital. Although there's a basic seaside appeal here and an attractive palm-lined promenade, the sandy beach, backed by a dense concentration of unruly apartment blocks, isn't one of the island's finest. Unlike many Ibiza resorts, there's a small resident population, and in winter, when the tourists have gone, elderly Ibizans reclaim the streets to stroll, chat and take the sea air.

Undoubtedly one of the most happening places in Ibiza during the 1950s (a collection of Dutch writers and artists spent several seasons here) and the focus of the early beatnik scene in the 1960s, there's little evidence today of Figueretes' boho past. Nightlife and eating options are plentiful but perfunctory, and the main draw is location – Figueretes makes a convenient and economic base for serious forays into the dynamic night scene just around the bay. Gay visitors have known this for years, and many return annually to the same apartments.

Hotels

El Corsario

c/Ponent 5, Dalt Vila ☎ 971 301 248, ⓦ www.ibiza-hotels.com/CORSARIO. This former pirate's den in the heart of Dalt Vila – a hike uphill from the port area – is now an atmospheric hotel. The rooms are small, but have plenty of character, with beamed roofs and period furniture, and many have dramatic harbour views. Note that the cheapest rooms have private, but not en-suite bathrooms, while the suites (€220–430) have more space, including a lounge. Eschew the overpriced restaurant. €130–160.

Hostal La Marina

c/Barcelona 7, La Marina ☎ 971 310 172, ⓦ www.ibiza-hotels .com/lamarina. Historic portside hotel in the heart of the action, so noise is an issue in high season. Offers stylish, good-value rooms – most have wrought-iron beds, air con and satellite TV – divided between three neighbouring houses. Many

> The **price range** given in accommodation reviews indicates the cost of the cheapest double room in high season (June–Sept) – note that prices may be even higher in August.

PLACES Ibiza Town and around

▼ EL CORSARIO

rooms in the main La Marina building have balconies or terraces, some facing the harbour. €77–100.

Hostal Parque

Plaça des Parc 4, New Town ☎971 301 358, ⓦwww.hostalparque .com. Totally renovated in 2007, this fine hotel enjoys a superb location overlooking one of Ibiza Town's prettiest squares and has a popular café. The air-con rooms are not large, but have very high quality fittings, fine bed linen, shower zones and flat-screen TVs. On the roof, the three suites (€130-170) enjoy private sun terraces. €70–100.

El Hotel

Passeig Marítim, New Harbour ☎971 315 963, ⓦwww.elhotelpacha.com. Owned by the club *Pacha* (see p.77), this large modernist hotel opened in 2004 to rave reviews. The huge suite-size rooms really have a wow factor, boasting Philippe Starck-style furnishings and bathrooms, their modernity tempered with rustic artefacts and tribal carvings. Style cats will love the über-hip lounge bar, but the decked pool area is disappointingly small and poorly situated. It's pricey, but winter rates are a steal. Breakfast is included. €260–386.

Hotel Es Vivé

c/Carles Roman Ferrer 8, Figueretes ☎971 301 902, ⓦwww.hotelesvive .com. May–Oct. Styling itself as *the* "hotel in the know", this contemporary place is a Balearic HQ for UK clubbers, with good connections to the main venues, and has even spawned its own CD series. On the plus side, there's an attractive decked pool area, two very hip bars (open around the clock) and fine food from a modish menu. But prepare yourself for small, if neat rooms, steep prices and a four-night minimum stay between Thursdays and Mondays. €150–235.

Hotel Lux Isla

c/Josep Pla 1, Talamanca ☎971 313 469, ⓦwww.luxisla.com. An excellent deal, this small, recently renovated modern hotel is located just behind Talamanca Beach, about 2km from Ibiza Town. The rooms are bright, attractive and

▼ EL HOTEL

▲ LA VENTANA

comfortable, most with balconies and sea views, and air con available as an optional extra. You'll find a decent café-restaurant downstairs. €66–115.

La Ventana

Sa Carrossa 13, Dalt Vila ☎971 390 857, ⓦ www.laventanaibiza.com. Enjoying a terrific, tranquil setting just inside Dalt Vila, this classy converted mansion's rooms and hallways come replete with antiques and exotic textiles. The twelve rooms are not large, but are equipped with air con and four-poster beds; most have great harbour views and some have balconies (€260), as do the two magnificent suites (€432). The pavement restaurant is one of Ibiza's finest (see review p.72), while the rooftop terrace is the perfect spot for a memorable sundowner. Rates drop by a third in winter. €173.

Pensions

Casa de Huéspedes Vara de Rey

Vara de Rey 7, New Town ☎971 301 376, ⓦ www.hibiza.com. A welcoming little guesthouse right in the heart of Ibiza Town, whose simple but attractive rooms are artistically furnished

with seashell-encrusted mirrors and driftwood wardrobes; most share bathrooms. Streetside rooms can be a little noisy in high season. €60–120.

Hostal Bimbi

c/Ramón Muntaner 55, Figueretes ☎971 305 396, ⓦ www.hostalbimbi .com. May–Oct. Backpacker-friendly *hostal* just a block from Figueretes beach and a ten-minute walk from Ibiza Town. Seventeen clean, orderly rooms with washbasins and wardrobes, two with private bathrooms. The management offer good local information and also rent out apartments closer to the centre of town. €46–54.

Hostal Ripoll

c/ Vicente Cuervo 14, New Town ☎971 314 275. A popular family-owned *hostal*, well-run by a *señora* who ensures the plain but airy rooms are well-kept and bathrooms (all communal) are scrubbed clean. €50–65.

Sol y Brisa

Avgda Bartomeu Vicente Ramón 15, New Town ☎971 310 818. Cheap, clean and friendly family-run place on a side street close to the port. The twenty rooms are small and share bathrooms, but are good value. €45–58.

Apartments

Apartamentos Roselló

c/Juli Cirer i Vela, Es Soto ☎971 302 790, ⓦ www.apartamentosrosello .com. Most of these spacious, comfortable apartments have wonderful sun terraces or large balconies positioned right above the Mediterranean with views across to Formentera. All (except the singles) have a bedroom with twin beds and a large sunny living area with two more day beds, plus full cooking facilities. The location is very tranquil, yet just a five-minute walk from both Figueretes beach and the heart of Ibiza Town. Very reasonable prices, especially outside high season, and an extremely helpful Ibizan owner. €79–109.

La Torre del Canónigo

c/Major 8, Dalt Vila ☎971 303 884, ⓦ www.elcanonigo.com. Easter–New Year. Highly atmospheric "apart-hotel", occupying part of a fourteenth-century defensive tower in a commanding position high up in Dalt Vila. Oozing character, the suite-sized accommodation has every mod con including kitchen facilities, satellite TV, DVD and CD players, while some even have terraces with a Jacuzzi. Guests have access to a swimming pool close by. It's a right hike uphill from the port area, though. €226–470.

Shops

Boutique Divina

c/Santa Creu, Dalt Vila. Ibiza is renowned for its home-grown "ad lib" fashion – characterized by loose, flowing white linen – and this boutique has racks of elegant designs.

Can Felix

c/Antoni Palau 1, La Marina. A diverse selection of wonderful traditional and modern fans and costume and beaded shawls at moderate prices.

Decadence

c/Bisbe Azara 3, La Marina. Small boutique with good selection of hip menswear, including the No2 label.

DJ Beat

Plaça de la Tertulia, La Marina. One of Ibiza's premier record stores. Racks of dance vinyl, and some mixed electronica and lounge CDs too.

▼ DJ BEAT

Envy

c/G. de Montgrí 22, La Marina. Very affordable boutique offering groovy, highly individualistic girly clubwear and accessories. There's a second branch right opposite.

Merhaba Ibiza

Avgda d'Espanya 43, New Town. Warehouse-style store, with racks of inexpensive women's boho garb, beaded sandals and beach wear.

Natural

Plaça des Parc, New Town. Specializes in jewellery and accessories with an ethnic flavour, scented candles and Indian cotton fabrics.

Noon

Caietà Soler 9, New Town. Über-hip boutique-cum-café with a good stock of designer gear, including Paul Smith and G Star. Also has Internet access and a coffee bar, and stocks a few fashion, film and music books and magazines.

El Secreto de Baltasar

Comte Roselló 6, La Marina. Stylish shoe emporium, with a great selection of moderately priced men's and women's leather footwear, including DKNY, Cryff and Bikkenburg. Also stocks some Miss Sixty bags.

Cafés

Chill

Via Púnica 49, New Town. Daily 10am–midnight. Ibiza Town's most hospitable Internet café, where you can chat, surf and tuck into a healthy menu of fruit salads and pitta-bread sandwiches. They also serve up huge frothy coffees, herbal teas, juices, smoothies, beers, wine and spirits.

▲ CROISSANT SHOW

Croissant Show

Plaça de sa Constitució, La Marina. Daily: April–June & Oct 6am–2am; July–Sept open 24hr. An Ibizan institution, just under the gateway to Dalt Vila. Come here for butter-rich croissants and pastries, revitalizing juices and fine *café con leche*. It's a quirky place, and the waiting staff like to club till dawn, so service can be patchy, or even negligent at times. For a takeaway, get your *bocadillo* and ice cream from the *tienda* next door.

Croissantería Jesús

Ctra Cala Llonga, Jesús. Wed–Sun 7am–3pm. One of the finest places for breakfast in Ibiza; pick and mix from flaky croissants, muesli, fresh juices, wholemeal toast, eggs and ham, or opt for one of the set deals. There's a pavement terrace and a cheery interior decorated with old Martini signs.

Madagascar

Plaça des Parc, New Town. Daily: May–Sept 9am–2am; Oct–April 9am–midnight. Perhaps the pick of the cafés on pretty Plaça des

▲ MADAGASCAR

Parc, *Madagascar* is stylish rather than self-consciously chic, and attracts a disparate clientele. Great juices (try the mixed carrot and fresh orange) and a limited food menu, plus very fine mocha-tinged *café con leche*.

Out of Time People

c/Jaume 2, New Town. Daily 9am–11pm. Veggie stronghold with an eclectic menu of global dishes including *tamales* (a Mexican snack made with maize) and Indian-style curries. Also good for breakfast or a fresh juice, and there are New Age books and CDs for sale too.

Sa Botiga

Avgda d'Ignaci Wallis 14, New Town. Daily noon–midnight. Chic and refined, this comfortable place features monochrome photographs and exposed sandstone walls. Has a well-priced *menú del día*, a tapas menu and some decent wines.

Sunset Café

Plaça des Parc, New Town. Daily 9am–2am. Stylish bar-café that attracts a loyal clientele, including a regular bunch of boho characters from the north

of the island. The striking decor combines animal prints, velvet and neo-industrial fixtures; the music evolves from chilled daytime tunes to electro DJ sets.

Restaurants

Bar Flotante

Talamanca Beach ☎971 190 466. Daily 11am–11pm. Highly enjoyable, inexpensive and informal café-restaurant at the southern end of Talamanca Beach where you can dine right by the waves and watch a stream of planes swoop down towards the airport. Offers huge portions, with good fish and seafood. Children are very welcome.

Bon Lloc

Ctra Cala Llonga, Jesús. Daily 7am–midnight. Unpretentious village bar-restaurant that's crammed in the early mornings with Ibizan workers downing brandy and *café solo* and puffing Ducados. Later on, it's ideal for tapas or a cheap set meal (€8) in the large interior or streetside terrace.

Bon Profit

Plaça des Parc 5, New Town. Mon–Sat 1–3.30pm & 7.30–10.30pm. No reservations. This place has hit on a winning formula, offering hearty, wholesome and reasonably-priced Spanish food in a canteen-style dining room, with shared tables. Main dishes (€4–9) include *dorada a la plancha* (grilled sea bream), and there's a short, well-chosen tapas menu (€3–6) too. The queues outside testify to its popularity.

La Brasa

c/Pere Sala 3, La Marina ☎971 301 202. Noon–4pm & 7.30pm–12.30am. Boasts an elegant garden terrace that's perfect for summer dining, and an attractive interior (where a log fire burns in winter). The moderately expensive Mediterranean menu is meat- and fish-based, with dishes including *arroz negro* (rice cooked in squid ink) and salmon cooked with lobster sauce – most around €20 – and daily specials using seasonal ingredients.

Comidas Bar San Juan

c/G. de Montgri 8, La Marina. Daily 1.30–3.30pm & 8–11.30pm. No reservations. Venerable restaurant that's been run by the same hospitable family for generations. Two tiny, atmospheric wood-panelled rooms and tasty, inexpensive (€3.50–10) Spanish and Ibizan dishes – *carne asada* (barbecued beef) – is just €3.90. You may be asked to share a table, particularly in high season.

Macao Café

Plaça de sa Riba, Sa Penya ☎971 314 707, ⓦwww.macaocafe.com. Daily: May–Oct 1–4pm & 7.30pm–1am; Nov–April 7.30–11.30pm. Deceptively modest-looking

Italian restaurant at the extreme eastern end of the harbour where the cooking is consistently good and prices are reasonable. Tuck into imaginatively prepared meat, fish and vegetarian dishes and particularly good fresh pasta. Popular with island-based and visiting celebs.

El Parador

c/Portinatx 2, Can Escandell ☎971 300 536. Terrific, very informal Argentinian-style restaurant located on the corner of the busy Avgda de Sant Josep road about 1km west of Ibiza Town. *El Parador* is all about meat; racks of beef sizzle and spit on the vast *parrilla* (barbecue), though all dishes come with chips and salad. Grab a table in the tiled interior or sit outside next to the highway. It's very cheap to eat here, around €15 a head including drinks, though little English is spoken.

Pasajeros

1st Floor, c/Vicent Soler, La Marina (no reservations). May–Sept daily 7.30pm–12.30am. Wonderful, frenetic and cramped first-floor French-Med restaurant that scores highly for value, flavour and taste, and near-zero for comfort – expect a long queue to share a table. It's highly atmospheric – the staff are all strong characters, and many of Ibiza's hardcore club crowd get their sustenance here. Try to bag the solitary balcony table.

El Pirata

c/Garijo 10B, La Marina ☎971 192 630. May–Sept 8pm–2am. Authentic Italian-owned pizzeria where you can eat pukka thin-crust pizza on a harbourfront pavement terrace. It's in the thick of the port-area action, so

▲ RESTAURANTS ON SA CARROSSA

a great place to catch the club parades and savour the hubbub of the Ibiza night.

Restaurante Soleado

Passeig de ses Pitiuses, Figueretes ☎971 394 811. May–Oct daily 1–3.30pm & 7.30–midnight. The finest restaurant in Figueretes, with a delightful seafront terrace positioned just above the sea, with views across to Formentera. There's an extensive Provençal-based menu with good fish and seafood and meat mains. Around €35–40 per person.

Restaurante Victoria

c/Riambau 1, La Marina ☎971 310 622. May–Oct 1–3.30pm & 9–11pm; Nov–April 1–3.30pm & 7.30–10.30pm. Charming, old-fashioned Spanish *comedor* (canteen), with simple furnishings and a welcoming ambience. It serves very inexpensive but well-prepared Spanish and Ibizan meat and fish dishes, and plenty of robust wines.

Thai'd Up

c/de la Verge 78, Sa Penya ☎971 191 668. May–Sept daily 8.30pm–midnight. Tucked away at the far end of c/de la Verge, this terrific little Thai place is great value, informal and ideal for a curry fix or a bowl of steaming, authentic *tom yum*.

La Torreta

Plaça de Vila, Dalt Vila ☎971 300 411. May–Sept daily 1–3.30pm & 7pm–1am. Of the many fine places to eat in Dalt Vila's Plaça de Vila, *La Torreta* offers some of the best cuisine, particularly seafood and desserts, though expect to pay around €50 a head. There's an extensive pavement terrace, or for a really memorable setting, book the inside room that occupies one of Dalt Vila's original bastions.

La Ventana

Sa Carrossa 13, Dalt Vila ☎971 303 537. May–Oct daily 1–3pm & 7.30pm–12.30am. Arguably the pick of the restaurants on beautiful, tree-lined Sa Carrossa, the menu here concentrates on Mediterranean and French dishes. Pavement dining doesn't get much better in Ibiza, with tables overlooking the city walls and a convivial buzz in the air.

Bars

Bar Zuka

c/de la Verge 75, Sa Penya. April–Oct daily 9pm–4am. Intimate and relaxed, this gorgeous little bar is a great place to meet and mingle with an eclectic bunch of interesting characters. The surroundings juxtapose antique mirrors and artwork, and for a great perspective of the harbour check out the "eagle's nest" balcony table. Mark, the English owner, was one of the original acid-house kids, and has plenty of entertaining anecdotes about the island.

▲ CAN POU BAR

Base Bar

c/Garijo 15–16, La Marina
ⓦwww.basebaribiza.com. May–Oct
daily 9pm–3.30am. Portside HQ for
a hedonistic crowd of (mainly
British) clubbers, dance-industry
folk and well-seasoned scenesters;
a raucous buzz surrounds this bar
all summer long. There's a large
terrace for alfresco quaffing, and
they're generous with the free
chupitos (shots).

Can Pou Bar

c/Lluís Tur i Palau 19, La Marina. Daily:
May–Oct noon–2am; Nov–April
11am–1am. Enjoys a prime
position by the harbourside and
has a quirky, disparate clientele
of Ibizan artists, intellectuals and
the odd drunk. One of the few
bars open in this area outside
the summer months. The
music is a mere
distraction as island
politics are discussed and
black tobacco puffed in
the wood-panelled
interior. Tasty *bocadillos*
are available.

Grial

Avgda 8 de d'Agost 11.
June–Sept daily 8pm–4am;
Oct–May Tues–Sun
9.30pm–4am. More of a
locals' local than a

tourist hangout, with DJs most
nights spinning everything
from indie to dirty electro.
With *Pacha* almost next door,
it's a key meeting point for
clubbers, and a good place to
visit in winter, when virtually
all the port bars are closed.

Montesol

Vara de Rey, New Town. Daily
8am–midnight. She's showing her
age now, but for decades this has
been the favoured meeting place
for Ibiza's moneyed classes.
Draws a mature, perma-tanned,
Gucci-toting crowd. Punctilious
service from immaculately
attired waiters, and prices are
surprisingly moderate.

Noctámbula

c/des Passadís 18, Sa Penya. May–Oct
daily 9pm–3am. Enjoyable, street-
chic Italian-owned place with
an outdoor terrace and a quirky
bar area that has plenty of dark
nooks and crannies. DJs mix
house and party vibes to a
sociable crowd, and there's a
little chillout zone upstairs.

Rock Bar

c/Garijo 14, La Marina. May–Oct daily
9pm–3am. Right next to the *Base
Bar*, its main port rival, this place
draws slightly older, more
international punters than its

▼ MONTESOL

PLACES Ibiza Town and around

▲ VAUGHAN OF THE ROCK BAR

neighbour. The owners have good connections to all the clubs (so free passes are sometimes available) and the capacious terrace is one of the prime places to enjoy Ibiza's long Balearic nights.

Teatro Pereira

c/Comte Roselló. Daily 9am–5am. Set in what was the foyer of a fine nineteenth-century theatre, this is Ibiza Town's premier live-music venue. Jazz bands, mainly playing covers, attract a sociable middle-aged crowd; entrance is free, but drinks are expensive. By day, it's a stylish café ideal for a tapa or two and a beer.

La Tierra

Passatge Trinitat 4, off c/Barcelona, La Marina. Daily 9pm–3am. Steeped in hippy folklore, this was the scene of major "happenings" in the 1960s. There's less patchouli oil around these days, but the ambience remains vibrant, carried by an eclectic mix of hard-drinking Ibizans. Musically, things are kept funky, and there are regular DJ sets.

Gay bars

Bar JJ

c/de la Verge 79, Sa Penya ⓦ www .jjbaribiza.com. April to mid-Oct daily 9.30pm–3am. *Bar JJ* has excellent links to the gay club scene, so buy a few drinks and you may score a complimentary pass. The attractive interior has great harbour views, and it's popular with a French and Spanish crowd.

Cheri

c/d'Alfons XII 3, Sa Penya. May–Oct daily 10pm–4am; Nov–April Fri & Sat 10pm–4am. Occupying the former premises of the long-running *Oriental*, this French-owned place is an ideal venue for catching the club parades. The drinks prices are slightly less draining than the neighbouring *Dôme*.

Dôme

c/d'Alfons XII 5, Sa Penya. May–Oct daily 10pm–3am. Gay Ibiza at its most gorgeous: stunning bar staff, horrifically expensive drinks and an ideal location, in the plaza-like environs of c/d'Alfons XII. As the final

▲ DÔME

destination of most of the club parades, the atmosphere on the terrace reaches fever pitch by 1am during the summer, when it's filled with a riotous assemblage of hipsters, wannabes and drag queens.

Soap

c/Santa Llúcia 23, Sa Penya. May–Oct daily 8pm–4am; Nov–April Fri & Sat 8pm–4am. Tight against the walls of Dalt Vila, *Soap* is a sociable place that's geared towards the

▼ CARRER DE LA VERGE

gay club crowd and renowned for its cocktails. Boasts a huge terrace, and also a small club zone (which used to be *Lola's*).

Sunrise

c/de la Verge 44, Sa Penya. May–Oct daily 8pm-3.30am; Nov–April Fri & Sat 8pm–3.30pm. A relative newcomer, this intimate place is Ibiza's only lesbian-geared bar, though plenty of gay males and hip heteros enjoy a drink here too. Run by a party-hard crowd, the *mojitos* here are superb.

Clubs

Anfora

c/Sant Carles 7, Dalt Vila ⓦ www .disco-anfora.com. April–Oct plus Easter and New Year. €10 until 2am; €14 after. Ibiza's only specifically gay club, *Anfora* is set inside a natural cave in the heart of Dalt Vila. It attracts an international, mixed-age crowd, with hip young urban boys socializing freely with homo clones and the leather posse. Musically, the sounds tend to reflect the disparate nature and ages of the regulars, with resident DJs mixing driving house with

Hitting the clubs

Timings vary from venue to venue and night to night, but most events start at 11pm or midnight and run till around 7am – exceptions are noted in the text.

camp anthems. The club's tiny backstreet Dalt Vila doorway is deceptive, as inside there's a large gingham-tiled dancefloor, a central bar and a stage (usually used for drag acts). Upstairs, you'll find a sociable bar area, and a darkroom which screens hardcore movies. Themed Madonna and Queen nights feature tribute acts. The door tax is very reasonable by Ibiza club standards.

El Divino

New Harbour ⓦ www.eldivino-ibiza
.com. Easter–Oct and some winter
weekends. Free shuttle boat from
Passeig Marítim (midnight–3.30am;
every 15min). €30–45. Jutting
into Ibiza Town's harbour,
with water on three sides, *El
Divino* boasts the most enviable
location of any club on the
island, its arched windows
revealing a panoramic view of
the floodlit old town across the
waters of the port.

Musically, the club
concentrates on mainstream,
vocal-rich house sounds, with
Hed Kandi, Defected and
Miss Moneypenny's installed
in the summer season (though
there are some gay and even
occasional psy-trance nights).
El Divino tends to draw a
label-conscious, cosmopolitan
crowd and the atmosphere
is usually sociable but less
explosive than the San Antoni
or San Rafel club scenes. For
those that like plenty of edge
to their music, *El Divino* could

be considered just a little
too smooth, the vibe more
"niteclub" than underground.
However, drinks prices are
fairly reasonable (for Ibiza) and
if you can bag a table in the
"VIP" terrace (just ask!) one of
the clubbing world's best vistas
is yours.

Heaven

Passeig Juan Carlos 1, New Harbour
ⓦ www.heaven-ibiza.com. €15–30.
Launched in July 2007, this is
the first overseas venture for
Heaven, London's most famous
gay club. The venue itself has
been a club premises for years,
operating under a bewildering
number of monikers including
Angel's el Cel and *Penelope*,
but spent most of the last
decade closed.

With a capacity of around
1500, perhaps the island's best
sound system, and a terrific
location overlooking Ibiza
Town harbour, *Heaven* certainly
has plenty of potential. The
capacious main room is
overlooked by podiums and
the DJ box, and there are bar
zones with sleek seating areas
as well as two outdoor terraces.

Initially, the owners offered
a mixture of gay and mixed
events, booking experienced
Italian promoters Zenith, with
big-hitters from the gay club
world filling other slots. But
many of these nights were
poorly attended, and PR people
were out in force in the port
bars offering complimentary
passes towards the end of the
2007 season in an effort to
boost numbers. So the jury
is still out concerning the
future of *Heaven* Ibiza: the club
certainly has prospects, but extra
investment is needed, coupled
with a commitment to working
with local talent.

▲ PACHA

Pacha

Avgda 8 d'Agost ⓦ www.pacha.es.
Easter–Oct, open Fri–Sat in winter.

Most Ibizans rate *Pacha* in a class
of its own; indeed when
referring to the club the answer
is simply "*Pacha es Pacha*". A
global empire – over seventy
*Pacha*s are dotted around the
world, from Marrakesh to
Buenos Aires – centred in Ibiza,
the island remains HQ for a
dance franchise founded on
chic, Balearic-style clubbing.
The club itself has a capacity of
around 3000, built in a series of
terraces that betray its origins as
a farmhouse, and the
whitewashed exterior of the old
finca, framed by floodlit palm
trees, creates a real sense of
occasion. Inside, the beautiful
main room has a sunken
dancefloor surrounded by tiers,
there's a salsa room, Pachacha,

a Funky Room, El Cielo, and a
dark Global Room where you'll
find more diverse experimental
beats, and hip-hop and indie
rock on occasions. Classy little
details are everywhere, with
Spanish tiles evoking a
Mediterranean theme, while the
elegant terrace, spread over
several layers, is a wonderfully
sociable, open-air affair, with
vistas of the city skyline.

Pacha's decidedly international
clientele embraces all ages, from
young Ibizans to still-swinging
playboys, wide-eyed tourists and
fifty-year-old salsa fans. Over
the years, the most successful
nights, including Erick Morillo's
Subliminal and Roger Sanchez's
Release Yourself have
concentrated on uplifting,
vocal-rich house music rather
than slamming techno or trance
– music that suits the crowd.

The east

Ibiza's indented eastern coastline is dotted with family-oriented resorts and sheltered coves. Many of the most spectacular sandy beaches, such as Cala Llonga and Cala de Sant Vicent, were developed decades ago into bucket-and-spade holiday enclaves, but plenty of undeveloped bays remain, such as Cala Mastella, the cliff-backed cove of Cala Boix and the kilometre-long unspoilt sands of Aigües Blanques – the place to bare all in the north of the island. Santa Eulària des Riu, the region's municipal capital, is a pleasant town that acts as a focus for the east coast's resorts and has a friendly, familial appeal as well as a lively restaurant strip, two beaches and a marina. Further north lie pretty Sant Carles and the hamlet of Sant Vicent, surrounded by some of Ibiza's most spectacular scenery: forested hillsides, sweeping valleys and rugged coves.

Cala Llonga

Buses #15 from Ibiza Town & #41 from Santa Eulària, May–Oct Mon–Sat 19 daily, Sun 10 daily; 10min. Boats from Santa Eulària, June–Sept 9 daily; 15 min. Heading north from Ibiza Town, the first of the *calas* (coves) on the east coast is the small family resort of Cala Llonga. Set in a spectacular inlet below soaring wooded cliffs, the 300-metre-wide bay has fine, gently shelving sand and usually calm, translucent water. The scene is slightly spoilt, however, by the lumpish apartment blocks insensitively built on the northern cliffs. There are full beachside facilities including sunbeds, umbrellas and pedalos, and a tourist information kiosk (May–Oct Mon–Sat 10am–2pm). As in many Ibizan resorts, the cuisine on offer here is a little uninspiring, with the *Casa Piedra* close to the entrance road to the resort the best bet.

Sòl d'en Serra

Just 800m south of Cala Llonga, down a bumpy dirt track, Sòl d'en Serra is a slender,

▼ SÒL D'EN SERRA

Transport

Getting around the east on public transport is fairly easy. Santa Eulària is served by frequent **buses** from Ibiza Town and is well connected to the area's resorts and villages by regular bus and **boat** services (indicated in the text). However, to get to the more remote beaches, you'll have to arrange your own transport – or take taxis.

undeveloped 500-metre-long pebble beach backed by high golden cliffs. The shore is quite exposed here, and the sea can get choppy on windy days – perfect for an invigorating dip if

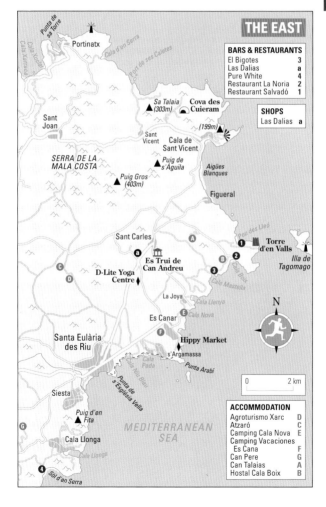

THE EAST

BARS & RESTAURANTS

El Bigotes	3
Las Dalias	a
Pure White	4
Restaurant La Noria	2
Restaurant Salvadó	1

SHOPS

Las Dalias	a

ACCOMMODATION

Agroturismo Xarc	D
Atzaró	C
Camping Cala Nova	E
Camping Vacaciones Es Cana	F
Can Pere	G
Can Talaias	A
Hostal Cala Boix	B

Arrival and information

Santa Eulària's new bus station is on Camí de Missa, a couple of blocks north of the Plaça d'Espanya. Boats leave from a dock on the west side of Port Esportiu. Between June and September they serve Formentera (2 daily day-trips, 1hr 15min one way, leaving around 9am and returning to Ibiza by 6.30pm), Ibiza Town (5 daily, 40min) and beaches to the north and south. There's a tourist information centre (May–Oct Mon–Fri 9.30am–1.30pm & 5–7.30pm, Sat 9.30am–1.30pm; Nov–April Mon–Fri 8.30am–3pm, Sat 9am–2pm; ☎971 330 728) on c/Marià Riquer and a kiosk on Passeig de s'Alamera.

you're a strong swimmer, but not ideal for small children. The beach never gets busy, even in high season; between October and May, you're almost guaranteed to have it to yourself. *Pure White*, the stylish bar-restaurant overlooking the waves, offers a globally-influenced menu including sushi and Med cuisine; it also has a terrace with sunbeds, and hosts occasional after-parties.

Santa Eulària des Riu

Bus #13 from Ibiza Town, May–Sept Mon–Sat every 30min, Sun hourly; Oct–April Mon–Sat hourly, Sun 7 daily; 25min. Bus #19 from Sant Antoni May–Oct Mon–Sat 5 daily; Nov–April Mon–Fri 3 daily; 30min. Bus #24 from airport, May–Oct 7 daily; 30min. Boat from Ibiza Town, May–Oct 5 daily; 40min. In an island of excess, Santa Eulària des Riu, Ibiza's third largest town, is remarkable for its ordinariness. Understated and provincial, the town lies on the eastern bank of the only river in the Balearics. Its best aspect, however, is its shoreline; the two town **beaches** are clean and tidy, with softly sloping sands that are ideal for children, while the marina, **Port Esportiu**, is a popular place for a drink or meal, with plenty of choice. The graceful **Ajuntament** (town hall), built in 1795 and sporting a stout-arched colonnade flanked by two simple municipal coats-of-arms, dominates the north side of Plaça d'Espanya.

▼ PASSEIG DE S'ALAMERA

SANTA EULÀRIA

ACCOMMODATION
Ca's Català	A
Hostal Rey	B

Església de
Puig de Missa
Cemetery
Museu
Etnològic
Market
Bus
station
Ajuntament
Tele
Centro
Taxis
Taxis
Police
Nacional
Club Nàutic
Beach
Port Esportiu

MEDITERRANEAN
SEA

BARS & RESTAURANTS
Café Guaraná	3
Pussycat	2
Sandy's	1

SHOPS
El Corsario Negro	a

0   100 m

Just below, **Passeig de s'Alamera** is easily Santa Eulària's most attractive thoroughfare, with a shady, tree-lined pedestrianized centre. In summer evenings, dozens of market stalls add a splash of colour here, selling jewellery, sarongs and tie-dye garb. There's a good selection of moderately priced restaurants on Carrer Sant Vicent, although nightlife is pretty tame; most locals and visitors content themselves with a drink in one of the bars along the palm-lined promenade.

Museu Etnològic d'Eivissa i Formentera

Avgda Pedro Guasch. April–Sept Mon–Sat 10am–2pm & 5.30–8pm, Sun 11am–1.30pm; Oct–March Tues–Sat 10am–2pm & Sun 11am–1.30pm; €2.80. Halfway up the small hill of Puig de Missa, the Museu Etnològic d'Eivissa i Formentera has displays based on Pitiusan rural traditions. The main draw is the museum building itself, a classic example of the traditional flat-roofed Ibizan *casament* house. You enter via the *porxet* (outdoor terrace), while the cool, beamed *porxo* (long room) that now houses the ticket office would have been the heart of the household for most of the year, where corn was husked, tools sharpened and *festeig* (courting rituals) held. Most of the exhibits here are either carpentry tools or musical instruments, such as oleander flutes (*flautas*) and *tambor* drums made from pine and rabbit skin.

All the other rooms lead off the *porxo*. Room 4 houses nineteenth- and early twentieth-century women's clothing. Downstairs, room 5 is a damp natural cave, perfect for wine

Coastal walk to Punta Arabí

From the seafront promenade in Santa Eulària, an attractive, easy-to-follow coastal path follows the shoreline northeast to the modern resort of Es Canar. The six-kilometre walk should take two or three hours, with plenty of opportunities for a swim along the way. Head east along the promenade and after about fifteen minutes you'll reach the rocky promontory of **Punta de s'Església Vella**. The path loops around the angular modernist Palau de Congressos, a new conference centre and theatre, and passes above quiet **Cala Niu Blau**, or "Blue Nest Cove", where there's a hundred-metre arc of fine, sunbed-strewn sand and a simple fish restaurant.

Continuing along the coast path, past a cluster of pricey-looking villas, you'll arrive at **Cala Pada** in about thirty minutes; the 200m of fine, pale sand and shallow water here is popular with families, and there are three café-restaurants. It's also a surprisingly well-connected beach, with hourly **boats** to Santa Eulària and Ibiza Town during the summer, when boat operators also offer excursions to Formentera.

Some 500m beyond Cala Pada, the path skirts **s'Argamassa**, a compact, fairly upmarket family resort where a scattering of large modern three- and four-star hotels loom over the shoreline. From here the path heads inland, bypassing the wooded promontory of **Punta Arabí**, which juts into the Mediterranean opposite two tiny rocky islets. It's then a ten-minute stroll into **Es Canar** (see p.83), passing the *Club Arabí* resort, where Ibiza's biggest hippy market is held. Bus #18 will drop you back at Santa Eulària.

storage, where a grape press, vat, cask and decanter are on display. The kitchen (room 6) is dominated by a massive hearth and chimney hood while room 8 has a huge old olive-oil press. Up another flight of stairs from the *porxo*, room 9 has fishing spears and a framed privateer's licence, the legal certificate granted to Ibizan corsairs by the Crown, authorizing them to attack pirate vessels.

Església de Puig de Missa

May–Sept daily 9am–9pm. Puig de Missa's 52-metre summit is dominated by the sculpted lines of Santa Eulària's very fine fortress-church, Església de Puig de Missa, a white rectangular building constructed – after pirates destroyed the original chapel – by the Italian architect Calvi, who was also responsible for the walls of Dalt Vila (see p.54). The church's eastern flank has

a semicircular tower, dating from 1568, that formed part of Ibiza's coastal defences. Around 1700, the church's best feature was added: a magnificent and wonderfully cool porch with eight arches and mighty pillars

▼ ESGLÉSIA DE PUIG DE MISSA

supporting a precarious-looking beamed roof. The church interior is whitewashed throughout, with little decoration apart from a series of images of a suffering Christ and a huge, typically gaudy churrigueresque seventeenth-century altar – the original interior was torched in the Spanish Civil War.

Below the church, just to the south, the cemetery is worth a quick look, thick with verdant foliage and spilling down the hill over several different levels. Amongst the predominantly Catholic monuments, one tombstone displays a Star of David, in honour of a member of the tiny Jewish community that has existed in Ibiza since Carthaginian times.

Es Canar

Bus #18 from Santa Eulària, May–Oct Mon–Sat 25 daily, Sun 14 daily; Nov–April Mon–Sat 5 daily, Sun 2 daily; 15min. Bus #L24 from airport, May–Oct 7 daily; 40min. Boats from Santa Eulària, June–Sept 8 daily; 20min; boats from Ibiza Town 5 daily; 55min. Es Canar, a compact resort of four- and five-storey hotel blocks, lies 5km across the well-watered plain northeast of Santa Eulària. The inviting Blue Flag beach, with a crescent of pale sand, is Es Canar's main attraction, offering safe swimming in its sheltered waters. Unfortunately, the accompanying tourist facilities – a strip of British and Irish pubs, souvenir shops and fast-food joints – present a less attractive picture, though the special menus and happy hours at least keep things economical.

Es Canar is generally a family-oriented place, where children are well catered for and nights revolve around

▲ HIPPY MARKET, ES CANAR

"Miss and Mr Es Canar" competitions and quiz shows. However, it's the vast weekly **hippy market** (May–Oct Wed only, 10am–6pm), held just south of the centre in the grounds of the *Club Arabí* resort, that draws most people to this part of the coast, when traffic chokes the area. There's little original stuff at the market, and most of the stalls sell similar overpriced tat and disposable-quality jewellery.

For details of excursions from the resort on the tourist train, see p.170.

Cala Nova

Bus #L24 from airport, May–Oct 7 daily; 45min. A kilometre north of Es Canar, around the rocky coastline, the wide, sandy bay of Cala Nova is one of Ibiza's most exposed beaches; its invigorating, churning waves are especially strong when there's a northerly wind blowing. The sands never get too crowded here, and there are sunbeds and umbrellas for rent, and a small snack bar (May–Oct).

▲ CALA NOVA

Sant Carles

Bus #16 or #23 from Santa Eulària, May–Sept Mon–Sat 4 daily, Sun 1 daily; 15min. Of all Ibiza's villages, the pretty, whitewashed settlement of Sant Carles, 7km northeast of Santa Eulària, is probably the one most steeped in hippy history. Beatnik travellers started arriving in the 1960s, attracted by vacant farmhouses in the surrounding unspoilt countryside; the village, and specifically *Anita's* bar, became the focus of a lively scene. *Anita's* remains open (see p.90), though these days *Las Dalias* bar (see p.92), nearby, is much more of a boho hangout – it hosts a Saturday market that's well worth a visit for the stalls of ethnic oddities sold by a merry bunch of tie-dyed traders.

The village **church** is a fine eighteenth-century construction, with a broad, arcaded entrance porch and a simple white interior with a single nave and a side chapel. In 1936, during the Spanish Civil War, the Nationalist priest and his father were both hung from the carob tree that still stands outside the church, after clashes with a group of Republicans.

Es Trui de Can Andreu

May–Sept Mon–Fri 3.30–4.30pm, Sat 11.30am–1.30pm & 3.30–4.30pm; open sporadically in winter, call ☎971 335 261 to check. €3.80. On the outskirts of Sant Carles, 250m south of the church, the seventeenth-century Es Trui de Can Andreu is a fine example of a traditional Ibizan farmhouse, or *casament*. The whitewashed cubist structure displays all the renowned design features of Ibizan style so feted by modernist architects. Tiny windows punctuate the house's exterior in seemingly haphazard places, while all the rooms have an organic character, with bowed sabina-pine-timbered roofs contrasting superbly with chalk-white, metre-thick walls. The prefix "es trui" refers to Can Andreu's colossal olive press, the house's most unusual feature, which is kept in the smoke-blackened kitchen. Several other rooms exhibit various Ibizan cultural curios: musical instruments, farming tools including threshers and ploughs, basketry and *espardenyas* sandals. You'll be escorted around the building by a member of the Andreu Torres family, the owners of the house; they no longer live here, but are proud of their ancestral home and are keen to point out its unusual features. All visitors are offered a glass of local Hierbas liqueur; you can also buy Ibizan wine here. The tourist train (see p.170) stops here on its "Environment and Culture" trip, which departs from Es Canar.

Cala Llenya

Bus #16 from Santa Eulària, May–Oct Mon–Fri 3 daily, Sat 2 daily; 25min.
Southeast of Sant Carles, a signposted road weaves 4km downhill through small terraced fields of olive and carob trees before reaching Cala Llenya, a two-hundred-metre-wide bite-shaped sandy bay. The low sandstone cliffs are scattered with white-painted villas but, with few big hotels nearby, the fine sands never get too crowded – you should have no problem finding a sunbed or umbrella for the day, and a friendly beachside café (May–Oct) sells snacks and drinks.

Cala Mastella

Heading north along the coast, the next beach is Cala Mastella, some 3km from Cala Llenya; the road descends to the shore via an idyllic terraced valley. Barely forty metres wide, the sandy beach is lovely, set at the back of a deep coastal inlet with pine trees almost touching the sheltered, emerald waters. It's an exceptionally inviting place for a swim, although watch out for sea urchins, some of which are fairly close to the shore. A tiny kiosk (May–Sept) rents out sunbeds and sells drinks (including delicious home-made *limonada*), but for a fine seafood lunch walk 50m around the rocks to the north side of the bay and the *El Bigotes* restaurant (see p.91).

Cala Boix

North of Cala Mastella, a wonderfully scenic coastal road meanders for 1km or so through pine forest, affording panoramic views over the Mediterranean below, before reaching Cala Boix, set below high, crumbling cliffs. It's a beautiful sliver of a beach, with coarse, darkish sand

▼ ES TRUI DE CAN ANDREU

PLACES

The east

▲ CALA BOIX

and pebbles. Three simple restaurants line the headland high above the shore – *La Noria* commands the best views (see p.91) – and there's a simple *kiosko* just above the sands for snacks and drinks.

Pou des Lleó

Inland of Cala Boix, a lone country road cuts northwest for 1km or so, past large terraced fields separated by honey-coloured dry-stone walls, until you come to a signposted junction for the diminutive bay of Pou des Lleó. A tiny, pebble-and-sand-strewn horseshoe-shaped inlet, surrounded by low-lying, rust-red cliffs and lined with fishing huts, the only facilities here are a tiny snack bar (May–Oct 11am–sunset) serving delicious grilled fish and cold beers, and the decent *Restaurant Salvadó* (see p.91).

Torre d'en Valls

A further kilometre east towards the coast from Pou des Lleó is a seventeenth-century defence tower, Torre d'en Valls, set atop one of the few outcrops of volcanic rock in Ibiza. The tower is in fine condition and has metal rungs ascending its exterior wall; its door is kept locked, however. There are panoramic views over the ocean from here, towards the humpbacked island of Tagomago.

Figueral

Bus #23 from Santa Eulària, June–Sept 3 daily; May & Oct Mon–Fri 3 daily, Sat 1 daily; 25min. Continuing northeast, the next resort is Figueral, a small, prosperous but slightly bland place, popular with French and German families. It hosts a clump of hotels, a mediocre restaurant or two and souvenir shops offering postcards and lilos. The narrow, two-hundred-metre stretch of exposed sand is swept clean by churning waves, but swimming conditions can get a little rough when the prevailing northeasterly blows.

Aigües Blanques

Bus #23 from Santa Eulària, June–Sept 3 daily; May & Oct Mon–Fri 3 daily, Sat 1 daily; 30min. The naturist beach of Aigües Blanques, or "White Waters", is separated from Figueral's slender sands by a short section of eroded, storm-battered cliffs. It's accessed from the coastal road towards Cala de Sant Vicent; look out for the sign in Castilian for "Aguas Blancas". The kilometre-long slice of dark sand here, interspersed with rocky outcrops and crumbling cliffs and buffeted by the ocean, is usually fairly empty, and the beach even offers a little surf some winters, although conditions are only ever ideal for a few days a year. Aigües Blanques is the only official nudist beach in the north of the island, and very popular with hippies, who gather at the *chiringuito* at the southern end of the shore – a favoured place to watch the sun rise over the Mediterranean.

Cala de Sant Vicent

Bus #23 from Santa Eulària, June–Sept 3 daily; May & Oct Mon–Fri 3 daily, Sat 1 daily; 40min. Ibiza's isolated northeastern tip offers some of the island's most dramatic highland country, dominated by the plunging valley of Sant Vicent, west of the resort of Cala de Sant Vicent, the only tourist development in this near-pristine area. Getting there

▼ AIGÜES BLANQUES

is an attraction in itself: driving the coastal road north of Aigües Blanques is an exhilarating experience, following the corrugated coastline and weaving through thick pine forests, with sparkling waters offshore. Three kilometres after Aigües Blanques you catch a glimpse of Cala de Sant Vicent, its sweeping arc of golden sand enclosed by the 303-metre peak of **Sa Talaia** to the north, and steep cliffs to the south. Unfortunately, property developers have filled Cala de Sant Vicent's shoreline with a row of ugly concrete hotels, but the waters here still offer some of the best swimming in the area. Minimarts, cafés and restaurants sit below the hotels on an otherwise featureless promenade, behind which stand the derelict remains of a **concrete house**, which served as the hideout of French assassin Raoul Villian after he killed the socialist leader Jean Jaurès in 1914 and fled to Ibiza. Villian lived here in near-total seclusion for almost two decades before he was finally tracked down and murdered in 1936.

Cova des Cuieram

June–Sept Tues–Sun 10am–2pm. Free. A kilometre inland from Cala de Sant Vicent, there's a paved turn-off on the right (north) to the Cova des Cuieram, an important site of worship in Carthaginian times and one of the most remote spots in Ibiza. Hundreds of terracotta images of the fertility goddess Tanit have been unearthed here, some of which are now displayed in the archeological museum in Ibiza Town (see p.58). Consisting of several small chambers, the modest cavern has had to be structurally strengthened after damage inflicted some decades ago by a treasure-seeking lunatic armed with dynamite. Inside, there's very little to see, though it's thought the stalactites could have been part of the cult of worship.

Sant Vicent

Ibiza's smallest village, Sant Vicent, 3km up the valley from the coast on the road to Sant Joan, is easily missed. It consists of only a handful of houses, and there are no sights except for the austere village **church**, built between 1827 and 1838, with a double-arched porch and an appealing setting in its own tiny plaza, with a solitary palm tree for company. The facade is unembellished except for a small plaque, which confidently proclaims in Castilian Spanish: "House of God and gate to heaven". Around two hundred metres downhill from the church is Sant Vicent's only other feature, an orderly, dark little bar, *Es Café*, which also functions as the valley's post office and shop.

Port de ses Caletes

A tiny pebbly cove, barely 50m across, Port de ses Caletes is reachable only along a tortuous (but signposted) road from Sant Vicent that ascends via switchbacks to 250metres and then plummets to the sea; it's a bumpy fifteen-minute drive from the village. With a ramshackle collection of dilapidated fishing huts as its only buildings, the cove is dwarfed by soaring coastal cliffs, and it's a blissfully peaceful spot, where there's nothing much to do except listen to the waves wash over the smooth stones on the shore or snorkel round the rocky edges of the bay.

Hotels

Agroturismo Xarc

5km north of Santa Eulària ☎971 339 178, ⓦ www.agroxarc.es. This new country hotel is extremely good value, with nine very spacious rooms and a suite (€165–195) that combine *finca* features (exposed stone walls and beams) with modern design and air con. All accommodation is set to the side of the main farmhouse, where breakfast is served, and there's a fine pool area. The location is pretty, unspoilt and fairly remote, but is quite flat, so the hotel doesn't have the views that other places enjoy. Mountain bikes are available for guests' use. €130–165.

Can Pere

1km northwest of Roca Llisa ☎971 196 600, ⓦ www.canperehotel.com. This exceptional rural hotel,

▼ AGROTURISMO XARC

▲ CAN PERE

perched atop a hill with sweeping vistas over pine forests and meadows, offers real get-away-from-it-all tranquillity just 7km north of Ibiza Town. The nine immaculate rooms come with air con and modish bathrooms, while the three suites (€172–230), all with separate lounges, are very spacious and boast real rustic-chic character. The pool area has been revamped in recent years and now has tiered stone terraces scattered with Balinese-style daybeds for loafing. Breakfast is included, and evening meals are available in the attractive dining room. Rates plunge in the winter months. €134–172.

Can Talaias

2km northwest of Cala Boix ☎ 971 335 742, ⓦ www.hotelcantalaias.com. Spectacular hilltop *agroturismo*, owned and run by British actor Terry-Thomas's son, with panoramic views to the east coast. A distinctive ambience pervades the place, the stylish decor includes Asian fabrics and quirky sculptures, while the lounge is distinctly gentleman's–clubbish with its leather sofas, fireplace, piano and polished dark-wood floorboards. The seven rooms and suites (the latter starting at €280) are rich in character and comfort and have air con and satellite TV, while facilities include a terrific sun terrace and lovely pool area. The hotel also operates as a working farm and plant nursery. A filling breakfast is included and other meals are available. €145–225.

Ca's Català

c/del Sol, Santa Eulària ☎ 971 331 006, ⓦ www.cascatala.com. May–Oct. Friendly, English-run hotel set on a quiet street in the heart of Santa Eulària, close to restaurants, shops and beaches. The twelve (mostly en-suite) rooms are comfortable and simply furnished, and there's a delightful courtyard shaded by palms, with a small pool and sun terrace. Breakfast is available (€8) and afternoon tea and cakes are served. No children. €75–96.

Hostal Cala Boix

Platja Cala Boix ☎ 971 335 224, ⓦ www.hostalcalaboix.com. For a budget base in the north of the island, this agreeable, good-value place has sixteen airy rooms (all with air con and TV) with either mountain or sea views. Best of all, it's right above wonderful Cala Boix beach. Rates include breakfast and half-board rates are available. €51.

Hostal Rey

c/Sant Josep 17, Santa Eulària ☎971 330 210. May–Oct. Pleasant, central, neat and tidy hotel. The twenty moderately priced singles and doubles are all en suite, and have fans – those on the upper floors also have distant sea views. Breakfast (not included) and snacks are served in the downstairs café. €53.

Campsites

Camping Cala Nova

Cala Nova ☎971 331 774, ⓦwww .campingcalanova.com. Easter–Oct. Just behind Cala Nova beach and a short walk from Es Canar, this is an attractive and popular site with good facilities and well-kept bathrooms. Prices start at €8 per person per night. There's also a selection of self-contained log cabins (from €46) and mobile homes (from €57) to rent, and a bus stop right outside.

Camping Vacaciones Es Cana

Es Canar ☎971 332 117, ⓦwww .campingescanaibiza.com. April–Oct. Popular with families, this site is close to Es Canar beach and has good facilities: a pool, laundry, security boxes and a bar/ restaurant. Prices for the cabins (summer from €25), caravans (from €50), teepees (from €15) and hire tents (from €7) depend on the season.

Shops

Lotti Bogotti

Local 9, Urb Ses Oliveres de Peralta, Sant Carles ☎618 900 128. May–Oct noon–9.30pm; Nov–April 11am–6pm. Terrific new boutique specializing in all things vintage, antique and customized. There's glassware (from 1950s Murano to old English pieces), vintage bags, ornaments, mirrors, silk dresses (including saris) and musical instruments. But the real wonder here is the range of unique jewellery created by the owner from hand-cut beads of Bakelite, turquoise, agate, mother-of-pearl, crystal, malachite, quartz and coral. Well worth a visit.

Cafés

Anita's

Sant Carles. Daily noon–1am. Highly atmospheric village inn that's much larger than it looks from the outside. Once *the* gathering point for northern Ibiza's hippies, *Anita's* still attracts a bunch of local alternative

▼ LOTTI BOGOTTI

▲ ANITA'S

characters and serves excellent tapas and full meals; enjoy them in the snug bar or on the vine-shaded patio.

Restaurants

El Bigotes

Cala Mastella. May–Oct daily; Nov–April weekends only. Food served at 2pm only. No phone reservations; essential to book at least a day ahead in person. With (shared) wooden tables set right by the water's edge, this delightful lunch-only place is one of the most idyllic spots to dine in Ibiza – it's just out of sight from the beach, around the rocks on the north side of the cove. There's not much choice: *bullit de peix* (fish and potato stew, with rice), grilled squid or fish, a basic wine list, but great Sa Caleta coffee. Count on about €28 per person.

El Corsario Negro

Port Esportiu, Santa Eulària ☎971 319 358. Daily 8am–midnight. Well positioned on a prime corner plot in Santa Eulària's marina,

this all-rounder serves filling breakfasts, pizza and pasta, Spanish and international dishes at reasonable rates.

Restaurant La Noria

Cala Boix ☎971 335 397. Daily 12.30–4pm & 8pm–midnight. Looking over Cala Boix beach and the Med, with tables placed under the clifftop pines, this informal, moderately-priced place serves up excellent seafood: specialities include paella, *calderata de langosta* (lobster broth) and *mero San Jordi* (oven-baked grouper with potatoes).

Restaurant Salvadó

Pou des Lleó ☎971 187 879. Daily 1–3.30pm & 7.30–11.30pm. Modest-looking seafood restaurant perched above a tiny fishing bay in a remote spot. Serves some of the freshest fish in eastern Ibiza and superb paella at fair prices – expect to pay around €30 per person including drinks.

Sandy's

c/Sant Vicent 25, Santa Eulària ☎971 332 210. May–Oct daily 1–3.30pm & 7pm–midnight. Once the prime watering hole for holidaying English thespians, today *Sandy's* is a good bistro serving French

▼ CALA SANT VICENT

PLACES The east

▲ LAS DALIAS MARKET

and Spanish dishes. Excellent-value set meals are available and there's an attractive interior, or you can dine alfresco at one of the pavement tables.

Bars

Café Guaraná

Port Esportiu, Santa Eulària ⓦ www.guarana-ibiza.com. May–Oct daily 8pm–6am; Nov–April Sat & Sun 8pm–4am. Stylish and sociable, this is Santa Eulària's premier bar-club, attracting Ibiza's best resident house DJs. It's got a great harbour location and showcases some live music events with rock, jazz and blues bands.

Las Dalias

Santa Eulària–Sant Carles road km 12 ⓦ www.lasdalias.es. Daily 8am–late. An Ibiza institution, this large, quirky bar, restaurant and venue

has a good-sized garden terrace and a slightly schizoid clientele of farmers and hippies. Hosts a quirky Saturday market (see p.84) and various weekly events: Namaste on Wednesdays is an Indian-themed night with vegetarian food and live music, while Sunday's Fly High is the only legal psy-trance party in Ibiza (and runs till 4am). Check out the website for details of upcoming gigs (everything from grunge to ska).

Pussycat

Passeig de s'Alamera, Santa Eulària. Daily 8am–11.30pm. Yes, the name's a throwback to a cheesier era of medallions and sports perms, but this long-running whitewashed bar remains an enjoyable locals' local. Occupies pole position on the seafront promenade, and is a great place for a cool beer or *café solo*.

The northwest

From the tiny cove of Cala d'en Serra close to the island's northernmost tip to the diminutive village of Santa Agnès to the west, this is the wildest, most isolated part of Ibiza. A soaring, almost unbroken range of towering cliffs and forested peaks, the coastline only relents to allow access to the shore in a few places. Just two bays – Port de Sant Miquel and the small family resort of Portinatx – have been developed for tourism. Elsewhere, the pristine and often deserted coast offers better hiking than beachlife, as well as terrific snorkelling. Inland, the thickly wooded, sparsely populated terrain is interspersed with small patches of farmland where olives, carob, almonds, wheat and citrus fruits are nourished by the rust-red earth. Only picturesque Sant Joan and sleepy Sant Miquel could realistically be described as villages, though all the other hamlets have a whitewashed church and a bar or two. Ancient rural customs, including water dance rituals at remote springs and wells, still continue, while traditional cuboid Ibizan casaments outnumber modern villas in many places. In the village bars the Ibizan dialect of Catalan, rather than Castilian Spanish, remains the dominant tongue.

Sant Joan

Bus #20 from Ibiza Town, May–Oct Mon–Fri 7 daily, Sat & Sun 2 daily; 35 min. Bus #21 from Santa Eulària, May–Oct Mon–Fri 3 daily; 20min.

High in the northern hills, the pretty village of Sant Joan (San Juan in Castilian) lies on the main highway from Ibiza Town to Portinatx, 22km from the capital. Though only a couple of hundred people live here, the village is a municipal capital and boasts its own modest little **Ajuntament** (town hall). Dominating the skyline, the eighteenth-century church, just off the main highway, has typically high, whitewashed walls and an arched side-porch. The slim steeple that rises slightly awkwardly from the main body of the building is a

Transport

In summer infrequent **buses** run to virtually every village and resort in the northwest from Ibiza Town, plus the odd service from Sant Antoni; but very few operate in winter. You really need your own transport to properly explore this region, though day-trips to the likes of Sant Miquel (see p.98) and Portinatx (see p.96) are definitely feasible.

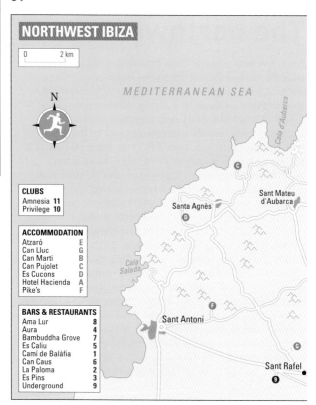

NORTHWEST IBIZA

0   2 km

N

MEDITERRANEAN SEA

Cala d'Aubarca

Santa Agnès

Sant Mateu
d'Aubarca

Cala
Salada

Sant Antoni

Sant Rafel

CLUBS

Amnesia **11**
Privilege **10**

ACCOMMODATION

Atzaró	E
Can Lluc	G
Can Marti	B
Can Pujolet	C
Es Cucons	D
Hotel Hacienda	A
Pike's	F

BARS & RESTAURANTS

Ama Lur	8
Aura	4
Bambuddha Grove	7
Es Caliu	5
Camí de Balàfia	1
Can Caus	6
La Paloma	2
Es Pins	3
Underground	9

Hippy mecca

Sant Joan first became a focal point for northern Ibiza's **hippies** in the 1960s, when a scene developed around the legendary Can Tiruit commune. Later the area served as a primary base for the Bhagwan Rajneesh cult (subsequently renamed the Osho Commune International), where elements of Sufism, Buddhism, Zen and yoga were blended with a good dose of hedonistic sexual libertinism. Rave folk history has it that Bhagwan Rajneesh devotees from California were the first people to bring ecstasy to Ibiza in the late 1970s, when there was the first mass ritual use of the drug on the island.

twentieth-century addition, which detracts a little from the wonderful simplicity of the original design. Inside, there's an unadorned single nave, with a barrel-vaulted roof and a small dome, comprising several segments painted with images of Christ.

Though once an important hippy hangout (see above), evidence of Sant Joan's

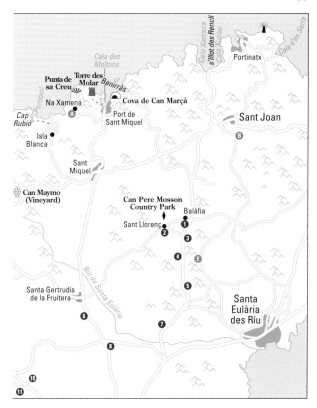

countercultural leanings is
somewhat muted today; the
spirit survives to an extent in
the New Age-ish *Eco Centre*
café in the heart of the village
(see p.106). The
region remains
popular with a
bohemian bunch
of artists and
writers, however,
and the remote
terrain around
the village is still
popular with
Ibiza's psy-trance
crews for
occasional parties.

Xarraca Bay
Bus #20 from Ibiza Town, May–Oct
Mon–Fri 5 daily, Sat & Sun 2 daily;
45min. North of Sant Joan, the
main highway to Portinatx

▼ CALA XARRACA

wriggles down to the coast, following a beautiful, fertile valley flanked by olive-terraced hills and orderly almond and citrus groves. The route affords sweeping views of the two-kilometre-long Xarraca Bay below, one of Ibiza's most expansive. Dotted with tiny rocky islands, the translucent waters are backed by low cliffs, and there are three small beaches. Four kilometres along the road from Sant Joan, a signposted side-road loops past some villas to quiet **Cala Xarraca**, a thin strip of coarse sand and pebbles no more than 150m long, with a few sunbeds and umbrellas to rent. The solitary bar/restaurant sells full meals and tapas, and is a fine spot to watch cormorants, and spear-fishermen diving at the end of the day.

A kilometre further along the Portinatx road, **s'Illot des Renclí** is a beautiful thirty-metre-wide patch of well-raked sand and very shallow, azure water; just offshore is the tiny islet after which the beach is named. There's a very decent fish restaurant here but no

snacks are available. A further kilometre to the east, tiny **Cala Xuclar** is a gorgeous, sandy, horseshoe-shaped inlet sprinkled with fishing huts, plus an excellent *kiosko* (June–Oct) for meals and drinks. The beach is very tranquil and the waters offer excellent snorkelling possibilities.

Portinatx

Bus #20 from Ibiza Town, May–Oct Mon–Fri 5 daily, Sat & Sun 2 daily; 50 min. Located on a double bay with three small sandy beaches, its well-spaced hotels and apartment blocks set between mature pines, Portinatx is a friendly, family-oriented holiday centre, with several other good beaches nearby. There's one stylish bar (*Zulu Lounge*; see p.108), but the restaurants tend to serve up standard-issue, tourist-geared fodder.

The larger of the bays, Port de Portinatx, has two golden patches of sand, **s'Arenal Gross** and **s'Arenal Petite**, where rows of sunbeds are rotated on an hourly basis in high season. The other beach, **Es Portitxol**, at the end of a narrow inlet

▼ BEACH AT PORTINATX

500m west of s'Arenal Gross, has well-sheltered water, perfect for swimming and snorkelling; there's also a dive school here (see p.173).

Things are pretty sedate for most of the year, but each July Portinatx hosts a three-day festival that includes an all-night beach party and beauty competitions and the like.

Cala d'en Serra

East of Portinatx, a very scenic road rises above Ibiza's northern tip, threading through woods and past isolated luxury villas. After 3km, there's a magnificent view of diminutive Cala d'en Serra, a remote, exquisite cove framed by green hills; it's reachable via a poor, signposted, but just about driveable dirt road. The only scar in the scenery is the ugly, half-built concrete shell of an abandoned hotel project just above the beach – though there are plans to convert the ruins to a spa resort here. The bay's alluring, translucent waters make an idyllic place for a dip, and offer rich snorkelling around the rocky fringes of the inlet; it's a short swim across to another tiny pebbly cove (also accessible over the rocks to the south). A café-shack (May–Oct) just off the beach serves decent seafood, *bocadillos* and drinks.

Balàfia

The historic hamlet of Balàfia is one of the most unusual settlements on the island, containing a cluster of ancient, interlocking whitewashed houses, and ochre-coloured towers where the population once sheltered from pirates. It's often cited as Ibiza's only surviving Moorish village, though the only definitely

▲ BALÀFIA

Arabic thing about the place is its name. Although there are a few *privado* (private) signs, there's nothing to stop you walking around the hamlet's two alleys to get a closer look at the houses and fortifications.

Sant Llorenç

A kilometre west of Balàfia, remote Sant Llorenç (San Lorenzo in Castilian) is one of Ibiza's least-visited settlements. The exceptional *La Paloma* restaurant (see p.107) aside, there's not much to the place – a village bar, a handful of houses and the large whitewashed **church**. A handsome eighteenth-century construction, it boasts a broad single-arched entrance porch lined with stone seating. Inside, the nave is topped with a barrel-vaulted roof, with a single nineteenth-century chapel dedicated to the Virgin Mary.

The wooded hillside above the church has been set aside as the **Can Pere Mosson country park**, a large recreation spot with good walking trails, barbecue areas and three lookout points offering fine views of the hilly heart of the island. The park is popular with Ibizan families at weekends, but deserted the rest of the week.

Benirràs

One of Ibiza's most idyllic beaches, Benirràs is a 300-metre-wide sandy cove set against a backdrop of high, densely forested cliffs. Development has been restricted here for decades, but in the last few years a rash of new villas have been built above the beach, despite a protracted campaign of opposition. Just behind the sands are three unobtrusive beach restaurants (open May–Oct and some weekends in winter) perfect for a seafood lunch or dinner with a view.

Legendary in Ibizan hippy folklore, and said to have been the site of wild drug-and-sex orgies in the 1960s, Benirràs's distinctly alternative tendencies persist today, and it remains the New Age community's favourite beach. Summer afternoons (particularly Sundays) see the bongo brigade gather here to bang a drum and burn herbs at sunset. At the mouth of the bay lies **Cap Bernat** – a prominent rock islet that's revered by the spiritually minded. It's said to resemble, variously, a woman at prayer, a giant baby, or the Sphinx – however, in the cold light of day, it's difficult to see what all the fuss is about.

Sant Miquel

Bus #25 from Ibiza Town, May–Oct Mon–Sat 6–8 daily; Nov–April Mon–Sat 3–6 daily; 35min. Bus #22 from Sant Antoni, Tues & Thurs 2 daily; 40min. Bus #37 from Santa Eulària, Mon & Wed 2 daily; 25min. Perched high in the glorious Els Amunts hills, Sant Miquel is the largest of the villages in this region. It's not especially picturesque – the

▲ ESGLÉSIA DE SANT MIQUEL

main street is lined with tiny old cottages that sit somewhat uneasily amongst five-storey apartment blocks – but it does retain plenty of unhurried, rural character, and you'll find a good mix of locals and visitors in the bars during the summer.

The settlement dates back to the thirteenth century, when the first walls of a fortified church were constructed on the Puig de Missa hilltop, a defensive position some 4km from the sea, giving the original inhabitants a little extra protection from marauding pirates. It's a short, if steep, signposted walk from the village's main street to the small plaza in front of the church, which commands magnificent views over the pine forests and olive groves, and has a small, welcoming bar. You enter the **Església de Sant Miquel** via the arches of a walled patio, then pass through a broad porch, which leads into the southern side of the barrel-vaulted nave. The frescoes of the Benirràs chapel, to the right of the altar, are the church's most unusual feature – swirling monochrome vines and flowers that blanket the walls and ceiling, dating back to the late seventeenth century, when construction was finally completed. Below the frescoes is some superb tessellated stonework in the form of crosses and octagons. *Ball pagès* (folk dancing) displays are staged in the church patio every Thursday all year round (May–Oct 6.15pm; Nov–April 5.15pm; €4).

Port de Sant Miquel

Bus #25 from Ibiza Town, May–Oct Mon–Sat 6–8 daily; 40min. Bus #22 from Sant Antoni, Tues & Thurs 2 daily; 45min. Bus #37 from Santa Eulària, Mon & Wed 2 daily; 30min. From Sant Miquel, a scenic road meanders 4km north through a fertile valley to Port de Sant Miquel, a spectacular bay that was a tiny fishing harbour and a tobacco smugglers' stronghold until the 1970s. Craggy promontories shelter the inlet's dazzlingly blue, shallow waters, and there's a fine sandy beach, but the bay's beauty is tainted considerably by the portentous presence of two ugly concrete hotel blocks built into the eastern cliffs. Catering almost exclusively to the package tourist trade, Port de Sant Miquel's bars and restaurants are pretty average – the *Port Balansat* is the best for seafood. In the summer season sarong and jewellery vendors set up stalls on the shore and pedalos are available for rent; you can also arrange boat trips to neighbouring beaches.

Cova de Can Marçà

Entry by guided tour. Daily 11am–1.30pm & 3–5.30pm. €5. Just past Port de Sant Miquel's hotel complexes, Cova de Can Marçà is a modest-sized cave system that, though unlikely to get speleologists drooling with excitement, is the biggest in Ibiza. The cave is about 100,000 years old, and was formed by an underground river that once flowed through the hillside. There are impressive stalactites and stalagmites, some sniggeringly phallic, and one that looks like a fat Buddha. An entertaining sound-and-light show ends the tour, with an artificial waterfall synchronized

▼ COVA DE CAN MARÇA

to cosmic electronic music from Tangerine Dream, who remain big in Ibiza.

Cala des Moltons

From the western edge of Port de Sant Miquel's beach, a path loops around the shoreline for 200m to a tiny cove, Cala des Moltons, where there's a small patch of sand, a good *chiringuito* (June–Sept only), and fine, sheltered swimming. The same trail continues past the beach for another kilometre, climbing through woods to a well-preserved stone defence tower, **Torre des Molar**, from where there are good views of the rugged northern coast towards Portinatx.

Na Xamena

Clinging to the vertiginous cliffs, and commanding spectacular vistas over the north shore, tiny Na Xamena consists of nothing more than a small development of holiday villas and the palatial *Hotel Hacienda* (see p.105). Nonetheless, if you're in the area it's worth a detour for the views alone, or for a quick drink in the hotel.

Swinging to the right just before the hotel, a bumpy road heads north to the lofty peninsula of **Punta de sa Creu**, where a heliport serves the rich residents of the luxurious houses here. The panorama from the peninsula is one of the most spectacular in all Ibiza; the jutting promontory is enveloped by the Mediterranean on three sides, and there's a brilliant perspective of the golden sands of Benirràs over in the east, and the mighty ochre cliffs around Portitxol and Cap Rubió just to the west.

Portitxol

Some 5km northwest of Sant Miquel, the hidden bay of Portitxol is one of the most dramatic sights in Ibiza – a fifty-metre-wide, horseshoe-shaped pebbly cove, strewn with giant boulders and dwarfed by a monumental backdrop of cliffs that seem to set the bay apart from the rest of the world. The only structures here are a ring of tiny stone-and-brushwood huts, owned by fishermen who use the cove as a sanctuary from the rough but rich waters, which plummet to over 90m in depth just a short distance from the shore. In high season, a few adventurous souls work their way to this remote spot for a little secluded snorkelling, but

▼ CLIFFS NEAR NA XAMENA

for most of the year Portitxol is completely deserted, a pristine – but also sunbed- and refreshment-free – zone. There's plenty to explore, however: tracks skirt around colossal yellow boulders of earth and rock, and past weird rock formations; the craggy peak that looms 315m above the bay to the west is **Cap Rubió** ("Blonde Capè"), named for its sandy colour.

Getting to Portitxol is a bit tricky. From Sant Miquel, take the Sant Mateu road to the west. After about a kilometre and a half, a turn on the right zigzags up through woods to the Isla Blanca complex of holiday villas. You pass a kiosk (open June–Sept), after which a rough road descends towards the shore – though it's so rough that you may well want to leave your car here. You'll soon reach a path that heads west by a high stone wall just before the second of two hairpin turns. Another twenty minutes' walk along the path, through some stunning cliffside scenery, and you're at the seashore, though for the very final descent you'll have to edge around the hillside for a short distance using the rope provided.

Sant Mateu d'Aubarca

Bus #33 from Ibiza Town, Mon–Fri 2 daily. There's little to the village of Sant Mateu d'Aubarca, 7km west of Sant Miquel, other than a confusingly aimless collection of lanes, a solitary but friendly store-cum-bar and a typically well-fortified whitewashed **church**. Completed in 1796, it has a fine triple-arched entrance porch and two tiny chapels, dedicated to the virgins of Montserrat and Rosario, set at

▲ SANT MATEU D'AUBARCA

the end of the draughtboard-tiled nave.

Tourism has barely touched the countryside around, a rustic landscape of small fields of brick-red earth separated by low sandstone walls. Much of the area is given over to **vineyards**, and on the first weekend each December, the village hosts an annual festival in honour of the humble local *vi pagès* (country wine; see p.177). Less than a kilometre east of the village, just off the road to Sant Miquel, you can visit **Can Maymo** vineyard year-round; it produces 25,000 bottles of red and white wine annually and, though they don't give tours, they will sell you as many bottles as you can carry home.

Cala d'Aubarca

Once the main point of sea access for Sant Mateu, the untouched bay of Cala d'Aubarca, 4km north of the town, is one of Ibiza's most magnificent. In an island of diminutive cove beaches, its sheer scale is remarkable: a tier of cliffs towers above the three-kilometre-wide bay, and a choppy sea washes the rocky shoreline. There's no beach, and as a result, Cala d'Aubarca remains one of Ibiza's best-kept secrets, completely deserted for most of the year.

To get here from Sant Mateu, follow the road "Camí d'Aubarca" from the church; after 700m, you reach a junction. Bear left and follow the road through a large vineyard until you pass a white house with yellow windows on the right. Turn right just after the house, up a dirt road that leads to the wooded cliffs above Cala d'Aubarca. Past the cliffs, the road is in terrible condition, and you'll have to walk the final fifteen minutes down to the beach. When you reach the rugged promontory at the bottom of the dirt road, look out for the natural stone bridge carved out of the rock by the waves. With the sand-coloured formations of Cap Rubió to the northeast, and brilliant white patches of chalk at the back of the bay, the multicoloured cliffs are also striking.

Santa Agnès

Bus #30 from Ibiza Town, July–Sept Mon–Fri 2 daily; Oct–June Mon–Fri 1 daily; 35min. Bus #30 from Sant Antoni, July–Sept Mon–Sat 1 daily; Oct–June Fri only at 8.15am; 20min.

Some 7km southwest of Sant Mateu, the tiny hamlet of Santa Agnès (Santa Inés in Castilian), is made up of a scattering of houses, a couple of streets, the simple *La Palmera* restaurant

Santa Agnès coastal hike

This circular walk (4.5km; 2hr) explores some of Ibiza's most remote coastal scenery, along high cliffs and through thick forest, and offers (if you're nimble) the chance of a dip in the sea.

From the church in Santa Agnès, follow the paved Camí des Pla de Coruna road west past villas, farmhouses and fields of vines, fruit and almond trees divided by dry-stone walls. It's fifteen minutes to the *Can Jordi* restaurant (May–Oct), where you can park and take your last chance to stock up with water. Just before the restaurant there's a rough dirt track on the right that leads downhill to the sea. Follow this, ignoring the first path on the left after a few metres, and continue down the track towards the waves, taking the next path on your left – it's about 200m from the road. This path continues southwest around the coastal cliffs, dotted with scrub pine and juniper bushes, keeping about 100m above the sea. The trail splits in places, but blue arrows mark the correct way, passing through the rocky headland of **Cap Negret** after another ten minutes' walking. Follow the blue arrows around a wall and continue through overgrown farm terraces before descending to a lovely clearing in the pines, where there's a long-abandoned farmhouse; the small domed stone structure was once a bread oven. Continuing west, you'll pass through a clump of giant reeds, then reach a series of large, overgrown farm terraces, propped up by substantial stone walls. Walk through the terraces past some old water-storage tanks. The route is very close to the sea here, but you'll have to scramble down the rocks for a dip. To return, blue arrows direct you inland up the wooded hillside. The steep route is a little ill-defined at first, but soon joins a dried-up stream bed before continuing up a pine-clad valley. After fifteen minutes the trail levels out and descends gently to the Camí des Pla de Coruna; turn left, and it's a five-minute walk back to *Can Jordi*, or twenty minutes to Santa Agnès.

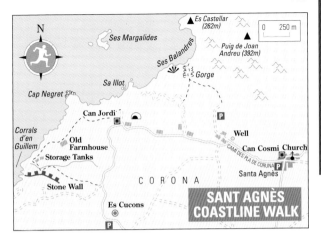

and the friendly *Can Cosmi* bar (see p.108). There are no specific sights other than the village church, which dates from 1806. It's properly known as **Santa Agnès de Corona** (Saint Agnes of the Crown) – a reference to its location in the centre of a two-hundred-metre-high plain, enclosed by low hills on all sides which form a crown-like surround to the settlement. With a patchwork of small, stone-walled fields densely planted with figs, fruit and thousands of almond trees, the countryside here is very beautiful. If you visit in late January or early February, the sea of pink-white almond blossoms is an unforgettable sight.

Santa Gertrudis de la Fruitera

Bus #25 from Ibiza Town, May–Oct Mon–Sat 6–8 daily; Nov–April Mon–Sat 4 daily; 20min. Bus #22 from Sant Antoni, May–Oct Tues & Thurs 2 daily; 25min. Smack in the centre of the island, 11km from Ibiza Town and just off the highway to Sant Miquel, lies Santa Gertrudis de la Fruitera ("of the fruits" – the village is known for its crops of apples, apricots, peaches and oranges). It's a small but interesting settlement with an international – and rather bourgeois – character, and offers a glut of bars, restaurants and boutiques out of all proportion to its size. Even in the winter months, tank-like 4WDs and ancient Citröen 2CVs compete

▼ AUCTION HOUSE, SANTA GERTRUDIS

for prime parking positions, and a collection of moneyed expats (particularly Germans), farmers, artists and artists–who–farm fill the streetside café terraces of *Bar Costa* (see p.107), *Es Canto* and *Otto Cappuccini* (see p.106). Besides the bars and boutiques offering ethnic fabrics, trinkets and handicrafts, there's also an excellent **auction house**, the English-owned Casi Todo (☎971 197 023, ⓦwww .casitodo.com; check website for auction days), where everything from Art-Deco clocks to gypsy carts go under the hammer once a month.

The landmark eighteenth-century **Església de Santa Gertrudis**, in the centre of the village, is less austere than most Ibizan churches, with an elevated frontage and small windows picked out with yellow paint. The interior, though hardly ornate, does have a few sculptural decorations, including, appropriately, some apples and figs on the ceiling. On the outskirts of the village, on the road to Sant Mateu, there's another chichi row of stores, including Nino d'Agata, a pricey boutique that specializes in jewellery and sculpture. The village hosts an excellent annual fiesta on November 16.

Hotels

Atzaró

6km south of Sant Joan ☎971 338 838, ⓦwww.atzaro.com. March–Nov. The biggest news in northern Ibiza for years, this spectacular new hotel retreat is centred on a 400-year-old Ibiza *finca* (farmhouse). Scattered around its extensive grounds are one of Ibiza's finest spas (with massage and treatment rooms and a

▲ ATZARÓ

sauna), a 40-metre lap pool and separate main pool, an open-air restaurant and lovely gardens, planted with jasmine, palms, cacti and lavender. Accommodation is divided between India-meets-Ibiza rustic-chic rooms in the main house, replete with Rajasthani wood carvings, and the sleek mod-Asian minimalism of the new block. *Atzaró* also operates as a cultural centre, hosting art exhibitions and musical and DJ events from the likes of local legend José Padilla. Low-season rates are very good value. €310–354.

Can Marti

2km south of Sant Joan ☎971 333 500, ⓦwww.canmarti.com. April–Oct. Unlike scores of other rural hotels claiming green credentials, this Swiss-owned *agroturismo* actually operates under strict environmental principles. Don't expect air con, hairdryers or a pool; instead you get a remote northern valley with fields of carob, olive, pistachio and walnut trees to explore, and organic breakfasts to enjoy. The accommodation comprises two doubles, a studio apartment and a cottage sleeping four (€240); all exude charm and a certain shabby-chic style. Rates include bicycle hire; very filling organic breakfasts are extra. €120–150.

Can Pla Roig

Sant Joan, just north of the church ☎971 333 012. This very inexpensive Ibizan-owned guesthouse has simply furnished rooms, with shared or private bathrooms; some have their own terraces. The guests' kitchen is a big advantage for euro-savers, and there are mountain bikes for hire. €38.

Can Pujolet

2.5km northeast of Santa Agnès ☎971 805 170, ⊛www.ibizarural .com. Rural retreat in a very tranquil location above Santa Agnès. The charming rooms have exposed stone walls, sabina-pine roofs and Afghan rugs as well as air con and modern bathrooms. There's a huge pool and Jacuzzi, but no restaurant. €202–235.

Es Cucons

2km southwest of Santa Agnès ☎971 805 501, ⊛www.escucons.com. One of Ibiza's finest country hotels,

enjoying a wonderfully peaceful setting in the high inland plain of Santa Agnès. All the fourteen rooms and suites (the latter starting at €286) in this converted seventeenth-century farmhouse are stylish and comfortable, with beamed ceilings, views and all mod cons including air con and satellite TV; some have fireplaces too. There's also an excellent restaurant, a pool and lovely gardens. Massages and beauty treatments are available. €240–268.

Hostal Cas Mallorquí

Es Portitxol, Portinatx ☎971 320 505, ⊛www.casmallorqui.com. March–Oct. Attractive beachside hotel in quiet Es Portitxol bay, with nine modern, comfortable and spacious rooms; all have sea views, TV, private bathrooms and air con or heating. There's a great terrace bar-restaurant facing the port with gorgeous sunset views. €86–110.

Hotel Hacienda

Na Xamena ☎971 334 500, ⊛www .hotelhacienda-ibiza.com. May–Oct. Ibiza's first five-star hotel,

▼ ES CUCONS

popular with supermodels and the seriously minted, is set in a spectacular remote location high above the rugged northwest cliffs. The rooms are commodious, most with terraces and a Jacuzzi aligned for sunset-watching, and there are four restaurants, three swimming pools and a gym. The sauna/spa includes a heated saltwater treatment feature complete with jets and cascades. Palatial suites are also available (from €751). Non-guests are also free to drop in for a sundowner. €336–376.

Cafés

Eco Centre

Sant Joan. Mon–Fri 10am–3pm & 6–8pm, Sat noon–2pm. Part New Age bazaar (complete with Osho music CDs and cactus-plant drums), part Internet café, and the place where northern Ibiza's hairy crew gather to surf, snack, sup and generally wallow in pre-punk nostalgia. There's a noticeboard rich with alternative info (like where to get sitar lessons or a raw-food workshop) and a lovely back garden.

Otto Cappuccini

Santa Gertrudis. Daily 9am–8pm. City-sleek café-restaurant, with contemporary decor (including a glass floor that showcases the artistic owner's remarkable terracotta seabed sculpture) and a short, tempting menu. Tuck into the à la carte breakfast options, including great fresh juices and pastries, or a lunchtime salad buffet (€8.50 per person). The delicious bread is baked on the premises and there's a well-chosen Italian wine list.

Restaurants

Ama Lur

Ibiza Town–Santa Gertrudis road, km 2.3 ☎971 314 554. Daily noon–4pm & 8pm–12.30am. Always very close to the top of the Ibiza chefs' own annual "Best Restaurant" vote, the renowned and expensive *Ama Lur* serves superb Basque and Spanish cuisine in a formal setting, with plenty of fish, seafood and interesting meat dishes. The waiting staff also really make an effort to look after the diners.

Bambuddha Grove

Ibiza Town–Sant Joan road, km 8.5 ☎971 197 510, Ⓦwww.bambuddha .com. April–Nov daily 8pm–1.30am. As a venue (a stunning pyramid-roofed bamboo-and-thatch structure) this place is exceptional, but the "Mediterrasian" cooking can be inconsistent. It's not cheap either – the buffet is €30, or around €45 a head to eat from the à la carte menu which takes in Japan, the Middle East, Southeast Asia and India. But eating here is still a memorable experience, with candlelit tables overlooking lush gardens, and a funky bar area with DJs spinning Balearic tunes until 4am.

Es Caliu

Ibiza Town–Sant Joan road, km 10.8 ☎971 325 075. July & Aug 8pm–midnight; Sept–June daily 1–4pm & 8pm–midnight. A carnivore's paradise, this affordable and comfortable country restaurant serves huge portions of grilled meat, and nothing else. The decor is rustic, with the odd stag's head or stuffed fox on the whitewashed walls, and there's a pleasant terrace for the summer months. Book ahead on Sundays.

Camí de Balàfia

Ibiza Town–Sant Joan road, km 15.4
☎971 325 019. Mon–Sat
8pm–11.30pm. A casual, cheap
family-run place that's
renowned island-wide for its
barbecued meat, sourced from
locally-reared animals and
cooked over the flaming embers
of olive and carob wood. Feast
on your carcass on the huge
outdoor terrace.

Can Caus

Ibiza Town–Santa Gertrudis road, km
3.5 ☎971 197 516. July & Aug daily
1–4pm & 7.30pm–midnight. Popular
with young Ibizans, this
inexpensive place specializes in
locally-sourced produce,
particularly meat, much of it
organically reared. You can
gorge yourself on dishes such as
cross-cut ribs or *sobrasada* and
butifarra sausages on bench
seating outdoors or in the snug
interior, and wash it down with
wine from the island.

La Paloma

Sant Llorenç ☎971 325 543, ⓦwww
.palomaibiza.com. An absolutely
wonderful country restaurant,
offering fresh, seasonal
Mediterranean food with a
modern twist or two. The menu
is changed daily and chalked up
on a blackboard, with inventive
dishes that reflect the owners'
origins in Italy, Spain and Israel.
Top-quality ingredients are used,
many of them organic and
locally sourced. Inside, the
dining rooms are intimate and
atmospheric, each finished in
sky blue and white, and there's
also a glorious terrace, snug bar
area and a deli-cum-store with
Ibizan produce.

Es Pins

Ibiza Town–Sant Joan road, km 14.8
☎971 325 034. Mon, Tues &
Thurs–Sun 7am–4pm &
7.30–11.30pm. A straightforward,
no-frills Ibizan restaurant with
log-cabin decor and a menu of
local dishes like the artery-
challenging *sofrit pagès* (a kind of
rustic Ibizan fry-up) and grilled
meats. All meals come with *pa
pagès* (country bread) baked on
the premises and garlic-saturated
alioli dip. The three-course
set-menu lunches are excellent
value.

Bars

Aura

Ibiza Town–Sant Joan road, km 13.5
ⓦwww.auraibiza.com. June–Sept daily
8.30pm–4am; Oct–May 7.30pm–2am.
British-owned lounge bar, with
a hip metropolitan vibe. Loaf
away an afternoon on the Deco
leather sofas, chill on the terrace,
delve into the premier-league
cocktail list or dine in style on
fresh, seasonal Med and
international cuisine. There's also
an adjoining art gallery that
showcases local talent.

Bar Costa

Santa Gertrudis. Daily 8am–1am.
Richly atmospheric village bar,
with a cavernous interior and
narrow, sociable pavement
terrace. Legs of *jamón serrano*
garnish the ceiling, while the
walls are covered in paintings –
most donated by artists to clear
their bar bills. Has a decent
menu and the most famous
tostadas in Ibiza.

Cafeteria Es Pi Ver

Sant Miquel. Daily 7am–midnight.
There ain't much competition
in Sant Miquel, but this
uncontrived village bar is
welcoming and serves decent
Spanish snacks, country wine
and beers.

▲ BAR COSTA

Can Cosmi

Santa Agnès. Mon & Wed–Sun
11.30am–11pm. Famous
throughout Ibiza for serving the
island's finest tortilla, *Can Cosmi*
is also a great local bar, with a
convivial atmosphere, plenty of
local characters, very moderate
prices and good service. The
elevated terrace is ideal for
summer drinking, with fine
views of the village church.

Zulu Lounge

s'Arenal Petite, Portinatx. May–Oct
daily 10am–1am. Your best bet in
provincial Portinatx for a stylish
bar, this place's alcove tables are
set under the rockface that
forms the rear of the bay.
There's an extensive cocktail
list, a menu of Mexican and
Mediterranean dishes, and
chillout sounds. It's underneath
the Es Grop apartments.

Sant Antoni and around

The club and bar-oriented scene in the package tourism resort of Sant Antoni (San Antonio) is as bombastic as you'll find in Europe. High-rise, concrete-clad and blatantly brash, San An (as it's usually called) primarily draws crowds of young Brits bent on a relentless pursuit of unbridled hedonism. Things can get pretty messy in the West End, with its unbroken chain of bars, disco-bars and fast-food fryers, but there are other sides to the resort. In recent years San An's Bar M has hosted a series of gigs by leading indie bands (including the Arctic Monkeys and Kaiser Chiefs) as the local music scene has moved away from mainstream club sounds to embrace other genres.

There are also plenty of less frenetic activities on offer. On the west side of town a burgeoning array of stylish bars line the new promenade, which connects the Sunset Strip with Caló des Moro. Sant Antoni's harbour, prized by the Romans, remains the resort's best aspect – a sickle-shaped expanse of sapphire water that laps s'Arenal beach, backed by wooded uplands. Around Sant Antoni, away from the crowded sands at the heart of the resort, you'll find some impressive cove beaches, as well as plenty of other gorgeous swimming spots.

Arrival and information

Buses all depart from the new bus station on the east side of town off Avgda de Portmany. Bus #3 serves Ibiza Town (May–Sept 52 daily, plus nightbuses; Oct–April 28 daily; 20min) and bus #8 also runs there, via Sant Josep (Mon–Sat 5 daily, Sun 2 daily; 30min). Bus #L9 (June–Sept 7 daily; 30min) connects San An with the airport. Boats (all May–Oct only) depart from the harbourfront on Passeig de ses Fonts.

Sant Antoni's **tourist information office** (May–Oct Mon–Fri 9am–2.30pm & 4–8.30pm, Sat & Sun 9.30am–1pm; Nov–April Mon–Sat 9am–1pm; ☎971 314 005) is on the harbourfront, just west of the Egg.

The harbourfront

Sant Antoni's main harbourfront begins at the **Egg**, a white sculpture erected to honour a tenuous claim that Christopher Columbus was born on the island. Inside the hollow structure is a miniature wooden caravel, modelled on the fifteenth-century vessels

PLACES

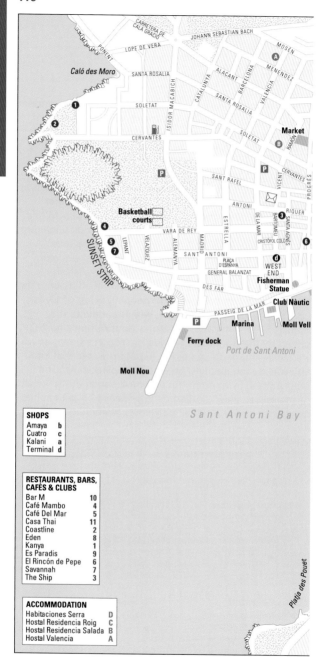

SHOPS

Amaya	b
Cuatro	c
Kalani	a
Terminal	d

RESTAURANTS, BARS, CAFÉS & CLUBS

Bar M	10
Café Mambo	4
Café Del Mar	5
Casa Thai	11
Coastline	2
Eden	8
Kanya	1
Es Paradis	9
El Rincón de Pepe	6
Savannah	7
The Ship	3

ACCOMMODATION

Habitaciones Serra	D
Hostal Residencia Roig	C
Hostal Residencia Salada	B
Hostal Valencia	A

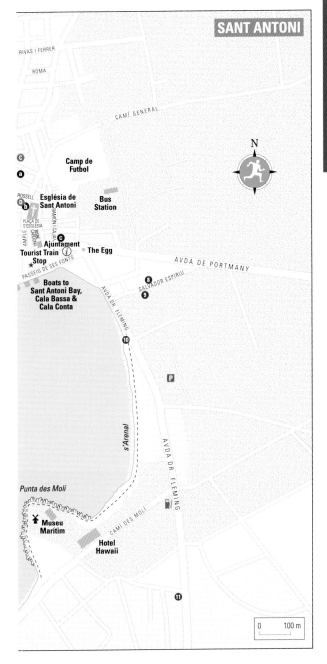

SANT ANTONI

PLACES

RIVAS I FERRER

ROMA

CAMÍ GENERAL

N

Camp de
Futbol

ROSSELL

Església de
Sant Antoni

Bus
Station

PLAÇA DE
S'ESGLÉSIA

Ajuntament

Tourist Train
Stop

The Egg

PASSEIG DE SES FONTS

AVDA DE PORTMANY

Boats to
Sant Antoni Bay,
Cala Bassa &
Cala Conta

SALVADOR ESPIRIU

AVDA DR FLEMING

s'Arenal

Punta des Molí

Museu
Marítim

CAMÍ DES MOLÍ

AVDA DR FLEMING

Hotel
Hawaii

0   100 m

in which the explorer sailed. West of the Egg, the broad promenade has a luxuriant collection of tropical palms, rubber plants and flowering shrubs, and a series of flashy modern fountains, dramatically illuminated at night. Behind the promenade, a string of concrete office and apartment blocks is occupied at street level by rows of pavement cafés, where you can eat American fast food or tuck into a full English breakfast while gazing at a Mediterranean harbour. On summer evenings, this area is lined with street sellers and caricaturists, and filled with drinkers.

The promenade narrows once you've passed a statue of a fisherman, complete with nets and catch; opposite here is the **Moll Vell**, the old dock, where you'll often see fishermen mending their nets and fixing reed lobster-pots. Further west, you pass the marina and modern Club Nàutic (Yacht Club) building before you reach a 400-metre-long dock that juts into the harbour, from where huge ferries head for mainland Spain.

Església de Sant Antoni

Just north of the harbourfront up c/Ample is the large Església de Sant Antoni, a handsome, whitewashed structure with a twin belfry and a pleasantly shady side-porch. The building mainly dates from the late seventeenth century, though there has been a chapel here since 1305. It has an unusual rectangular defence tower built into its southeast flank; until the early nineteenth century, cannons were mounted at its top to defend the town from marauding pirates. You approach the church through the twin arches of a cobbled, courtyard-like patio, with an elegant columned porch to the left. The sombre interior has little decoration, though some dark oil paintings of saints line the nave. The gilded altar replaced a previous Baroque piece destroyed during the Spanish Civil War.

The West End

The island's most raucous bar zone, the notorious West End – described by writer Paul Richardson as "The Blackpool of Ibiza, cheerfully vulgar,

▼ BELLTOWER, EGLÉSIA DE SANT ANTONI

▲ BOOZE GALORE, THE WEST END

unashamedly unglamorous"
– spreads over a network of
streets centred around c/Santa
Agnès. There's nothing subtle
about this almost entirely British
enclave of wall-to-wall disco-
bars and pubs, interspersed with
the odd hole-in-the-wall kebab
joint or Chinese restaurant
serving fry-up breakfasts. In
summer the streets are overrun
with sunburnt teenagers in
football shirts; understandably,
few Ibizans would dream of
drinking around here and you'll
be able to tell straight away if it's
the kind of place you'll love or
hate. In general drinks are much
cheaper than Sunset Strip or
Ibiza Town averages, and as the
disco-bars are usually free, it's an
inexpensive place to strut your
stuff. The music is generally
party-anthem holiday house and
mainstream R&B, but plenty of
decent DJs have cut their teeth
in the better bars, which include
Hush and *Rehab*, both on
c/Santa Agnès.

The Sunset Strip

Stretching for 250m along
the rocky shoreline between
c/General Balanzat and c/Vara
de Rey, Sant Antoni's legendary
Sunset Strip of chillout
bars is the resort at its most
sophisticated. A graceful new
promenade extends across the
coastal rocks, and bars here now
have attractive new terraces.
The location can be captivating
around sunset, when all eyes
turn west to watch the sun
sinking into the blood-red sea,
to a background of ambient
soundscapes.

Until 1993, there was only
one chillout bar, the ground-
breaking *Café del Mar* (see
p.124), along this entire stretch
of coast, and it was very
much the preserve of in-the-
know clubbers and islanders.
But since then the scene has
proliferated and there now
are half a dozen such bars
here, with the sunset spectacle
now very much part of most
people's "Ibiza experience".

It's undeniable that the
original sunset vibe has been
considerably diluted. The hype
is incredible in the height of
summer, when thousands of
visitors congregate, television
crews stalk the strip and
webcams beam the sunset

The San An scene

San An's importance as a breeding ground for **dance music** talent is undeniable. All the main players who kickstarted the UK's acid house revolution in 1987 holidayed in the town, soaking up inspiration at key venues such as the *Project* and *Milk* bars, which became bases for Chicago house music and Detroit techno at a time when the bars and clubs in virtually every other European resort were still playing party chart hits. Seduced by the spirit and vitality of the scene in San An and at *Amnesia* (see p.125), the likes of Paul Oakenfold and Danny Rampling sought to re-create the energy back in London.

Meanwhile, the more eclectic cinematic sounds championed by José Padilla at the *Café del Mar* (see p.124) became the focus for an Ibizan **chillout scene** and CD series that influenced key producers and musicians all over the world, establishing Ibiza as a nerve centre of electronic music.

By the mid-1990s, as clubbing became much more of a mainstream phenomenon, Ibiza's clubbing kudos and reputation for musical authenticity drew young British holidaymakers en masse to party in San An and experience the island's **unique scene**. The resort enjoyed its best years around the millennium, when over a dozen key UK clubs decamped to Ibiza for the summer and established residencies in San An and elsewhere on the island.

But by 2003 the music had become pretty lifeless, with an army of wannabe DJs playing near-identical low-grade funky house mixes and the innovation unleashed by acid house conspicuous by its absence. Enter Manumission, who, in typically provocative manner, declared "guitars are the new turntables", before announcing a summer season called Ibiza Rocks, featuring the cream of emerging indie talent from the UK. Then in 2007, with a terrific roster of bands booked to play at San An's *Bar M* (see p.123) including the Arctic Monkeys and Kaiser Chiefs, the authorities pulled the plug on the fun, declaring the venue didn't have the correct license for live gigs. Shows were cancelled or rescheduled elsewhere leaving fans furious, promoters frustrated, the authorities looking dumb and the reputation of San An as the cradle of an exciting new alternative rock scene in tatters.

The resort certainly has plenty going for it as a venue for live music and indie sounds, with Ibiza Rocks generating a mountain of publicity in the UK press, but promoters like Manumission will need to cement a strong working relationship with the local municipality for the town to develop into an Ibizan Camden Town.

scene around the globe. The commercialism is unavoidable – all the bars now sell their own T-shirts and CD mixes – but in spite of these changes, a certain unique atmosphere does survive, especially early and late in the summer season, when things are less high-octane.

Caló des Moro

North of the Sunset Strip, the new promenade continues for some 500m to Caló des Moro, a tiny cove with a small patch of sand surrounded by a scattering of hotel and apartment blocks. The opening of several swanky new bar-restaurants here has helped Caló des Moro become San An's most happening location in recent years, rivalling the Sunset Strip as *the* premier chillout zone. The bay makes an inviting place for a dip, with shallow, turquoise water. However, most people choose to patronize the swimming pools of the landmark shoreside bars at the sweeping

▲ CALÓ DES MORO

modernist *Coastline* and the neighbouring *Kanya*.

s'Arenal

South of the Egg, slimline s'Arenal beach hugs the shore as far as the Punta des Molí promontory. Though not the best beach in the area, it's the nearest one to town and the sands get very busy in summer. A section of the sea is partitioned off from jetskiers and boats so that swimmers can enjoy themselves safely, while bordering the beach are some stylish bar-cafés including *Bar M* (see p.123). A landscaped, palm-lined harbourside promenade runs along the back of the bay.

Punta des Molí

Jutting into the harbourfront at the southern end of the promenade, past a row of block-like hotel complexes, an imposing, old white windmill with warped wooden sails crowns the Punta des Molí promontory. This quiet, landscaped spot is planted with olive trees, lavender and rosemary bushes and is the site of the island's planned Museu Marítim (of uncertain opening date). Beside the fenced-off museum enclave, there's a restored well and an old water wheel, and panoramic views over the entire Sant Antoni Bay.

Cala Gració

A kilometre northwest of Caló des Moro, around the rocky fringes of Sant Antoni Bay, is the small but gorgeous beach of Cala Gració, an elongated patch of fine white sand which stretches back 100m from the sea. The shallow water is wonderfully calm and clear, and only gets really busy at the height of summer. A small snack bar (May–Oct) rents out pedalos, sunbeds and umbrellas.

A new extension of San An's promenade should reach the bay by the 2008 season, opening up access to a delightful section of the coast.

Aquarium Cap Blanc

Cala Gració is home to the modest Aquarium Cap

▼ VIEW FROM PUNTA DE SA GALERA

SANT ANTONI BAY

RESTAURANTS, BARS, CAFÉS & CLUBS	
Cala Salada	1
Can Pujol	5
El Chiringuito	2
Kumharas	4
Sa Capella	3
Summun	6
Sunset Ashram	7

ACCOMMODATION	
Camping Cala Bassa	C
Camping Sant Antoni	B
Hostal La Torre	A

MEDITERRANEAN SEA

Conillera

CALA D'HORT NATURAL PARK

Torre d'en Rovira

Cala Roja

Cala Bassa

Port des Torrent

s'Illa des Bosc

Cala Compte

Jivana Ashram Yoga Centre

Racó d'en Xic

Punta de s'Embacador

Cala Codolar

Blanc (daily 10.30am–7pm; €3), set in an old smugglers' cave on the south side of the bay. The centre is home to a collection of sluggish-looking Mediterranean sea life, including lobster, moray eel, wrasse and octopus. It's well organized and popular with children, with wooden walkways above pools containing the sea creatures.

Cala Gracioneta

Bus #1 from Sant Antoni, May–Oct 12 daily; 10min. From the fishing huts on the north side of Cala Gració, a path clings to the shoreline, leading after 100m to a second hidden bay, the exceptionally beautiful and peaceful Cala Gracioneta. This little gem of a beach is barely 30m wide, but has exquisite pale sand, backed by pines; the shallow, sheltered waters here heat up to almost bathtub temperatures by late summer. The bay also boasts a decent restaurant, *El Chiringuito* (see p.123), where food is served practically on the sand.

North from Cala Gracioneta, the isolated bay of Punta de sa Galera (also known as Cala Yoga) is popular with naturists

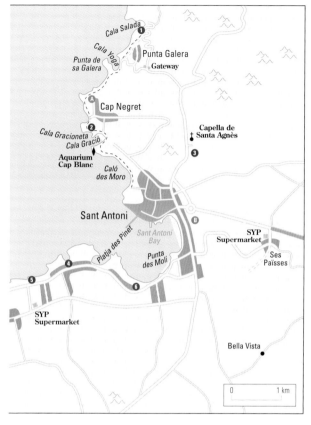

and hippies. Bizarre eroded cliffs of stratified stone and a series of shelf-like rock terraces (many painted with New Age doodles) form natural shelves for sunbathing, and the sapphire waters offer excellent snorkelling. In summer, a costumeless hippy sells cool drinks from an icebox most afternoons, and there's even a reiki masseur and reflexologist here, available (in theory) daily from 7pm to 8pm. To get to Cala Yoga by road, take the Cala Salada turn-off from the Sant Antoni–Santa Agnès highway, continue downhill until you reach a white arched gateway across the road, where the road splits, then bear left downhill towards the sea.

Cala Salada

Ringed by a protective barrier of steep, pine-clad hills, the small cove-beach of Cala Salada makes an idyllic escape from the crowds of Sant Antoni, with inviting turquoise waters lapping against a lovely 100m strip of sand. Apart from a line of stick-and-thatch fishermen's huts, a solitary villa and a simple seafood restaurant, *Cala Salada* (May–Oct daily;

▲ SUNSET AT CALA SALADA

Nov–April Sat & Sun), popular with locals, there's nothing here but the sea and beach. It is, however, one of the best places in the Pitiuses to watch the sunset, ideally in winter, when the sun sinks into the ocean between the gateway-like outlines of the islands of Conillera and Bosc.

To the north of Cala Salada, about two hundred metres across the bay, is an even more peaceful sandy cove, Cala Saldeta – you can either swim over or follow a path that winds around the fishing huts.

Sant Antoni Bay

Buses #2 and #6 from Sant Antoni, May–Oct 25 daily plus hourly nightbuses; Nov–April 20 daily; 20min. Boats from Sant Antoni, May–Oct hourly; 5–15min. Officially, the urban limits of Sant Antoni end at the Punta des Molí (see p.115). Continuing west, you enter the town's bay area, which is a little less built-up. Plenty of British visitors booked on last-minute deals end up in hotels around here, and though this strip is unremittingly touristy, it tends to attract more families than San An itself, and the atmosphere is correspondingly less boisterous.

From the Punta des Molí promontory, c/de Cala de Bou heads west around the bay, between apartment and hotel blocks and the attendant commercial sprawl. The best beach on this stretch is **Platja des Pinet** (or Platja d'en Xinxó), some 3km west of Punta des Molí. It's certainly nothing special – a small sandy cove, barely 100m wide – but offers safe swimming in sheltered waters and three cheap shoreside snack bars. It's possible to waterski or take a ride on an inflatable banana here, and there's also a rickety-looking waterslide complex (May–Oct 9am–7pm; two rides €1.20, ten rides €4). The coastal road around Sant Antoni Bay comes to a halt at the pretty, sandy cove of **Port des Torrent**, named after a seasonal stream which originates on Ibiza's highest peak, Sa Talaiassa (see p.131), and empties into the small bay. Nestled at the end of a deep inlet, Port des Torrent's sands are packed with families lounging on sunbeds and splashing about in the calm water during the summer, when a snack bar-restaurant also opens; for the rest of the year, it's empty save for the odd fisherman.

Cala Bassa

Buses #2 from Sant Antoni, May–Oct 8 daily; 25min. Boats from Sant Antoni, May–Oct 5–7 daily; 25min.
Cala Bassa is one of the most popular beaches in the Sant Antoni area: a fine, 250-metre-wide sandy beach set in a striking horseshoe-shaped bay, ringed by low cliffs and sabina pines. There are plenty of sunbeds and umbrellas to rent and three large café-restaurants, as well as a wonderful view of the hump-shaped coastal outcrop of Cap Nunó and the wooded hills of the island's northwest. The sparkling waters have been awarded Blue Flag status and there are plenty of watersports on offer, from waterskiing to banana rides, as well as a roped-off area for swimmers. Cala Bassa does tend to get very busy in high season, but peace returns and the beach clears by 7pm, when the last buses and boats depart.

Cala Compte and around

Bus #4 from Sant Antoni, June–Oct 7 daily; 25min. Boats from Sant Antoni, May–Oct 5–7 daily; 35min.
After a three-kilometre loop around the remote rocky coastline of western Ibiza, the Cala Compte road ends at the exposed beach of Cala Compte (Cala Conta in Castilian) which is generally considered one of Ibiza's very best. Though there are only two small patches of golden sand, it's easy to see why people rave about the place – and fill it with beach towels and hubbub during high summer – with its gin-clear water, superb ocean vistas and spectacular sunsets. There's also the added attraction of the new *Sunset Ashram* café-restaurant (see p.123) behind the sands, offering healthy food and a relaxed vibe.

Just to the south is the inlet of Racó d'en Xic, where there are two more tiny sandy bays, one popular with naturists that has its own *chiringuito* for snacks. The island directly offshore is called **s'Illa des Bosc**, "Island of Woods", though it's now completely deforested, the trees having been felled for charcoal burning over a century ago. The 400-metre channel-hop to the island should only be undertaken when conditions are calm – and even then only by strong swimmers – as swift currents can sweep along this section of the coast.

The much larger island of **Conillera**, just north of s'Illa des Bosc, is visible from most points of Sant Antoni Bay, from where its elongated profile resembles a giant beached whale. Many local legends are attached to the island – it's said to have been the birthplace of Hannibal and also to be the best source of the *beleño blanco* psychoactive herb, collected by pagan practitioners each year and burned during the night of Sant Joan (see p.176). Topped by a lighthouse, the island is uninhabited today.

▼ WATERSPORTS AT CALA BASSA

Cala Codolar

Bus #4 from Sant Antoni, May–Oct 4 daily; 30min. About 2km south of Cala Compte, minuscule Cala Codolar is very pretty indeed, with pale sand and clear waters sheltered by the rocky headland to the north, though it can get crowded in high season with tourists from the *Club Delfín* hotel just above the bay. There's a good seafood restaurant, *Restaurant Amarant*, and a windsurfing school, both open between May and October only.

Sant Rafel

Bus #3 from Ibiza Town or Sant Antoni May–Sept 58 daily plus nightbuses; Oct–April 30 daily; 15min. See map, pp.94–95. Perched atop the central hills midway between Sant Antoni and Ibiza Town, the fairly featureless village of Sant Rafel is all but overshadowed by the mighty clubbing temples of *Amnesia* and *Privilege* close by to the south. As part of a vast recent road-building programme (see p.121), meanwhile, a tunnel has been bored beneath the village, meaning San Raf is easy to miss from the main cross-island highway.

The village does have a decent assortment of stores and cafés and several good restaurants, mostly strung out along its modest high street. There are also a number of ceramic workshops on the main drag, and pieces are usually on show at the annual October 24 *fiesta*. Around 300m east of the high street, the nicest part of the village is centred around the **church**. Built between 1786 and 1797, it's typically Ibizan, with metre-thick whitewashed walls visible for miles around, and impressive buttresses. From the churchyard there are stunning views down to Dalt Vila and the sea.

Hotels

Can Lluc

Sant Rafel–Santa Agnès road, km 2 ☎971 198 673, ⊛www.canlluc .com. See map, pp.94–95. Set in a converted Ibizan *finca*, this luxurious rural retreat offers sumptuous accommodation. Most of the twelve rooms have exposed stone walls and beams, while all have CD players, air

▼ CALA CODOLAR

Highway to hell

Provoking the biggest public demonstrations in Ibiza's history (which saw 22,500 people, around 20 percent of the island's population, take to the streets in February 2006), the expansion of Ibiza's highway network not only caused public outrage but threatened to split the island in two along the new San Antoni–Ibiza Town motorway.

While most islanders agreed that the highway (previously one of Europe's most dangerous) had to be improved, protestors led by the Plataforma Anti-Autopista felt the €400 million new road network to be totally inappropriate for the size of the island. Allegations that the construction lobby and supporters of the centre-right Partido Popular (PP) were set to gain millions in contracts and compensation payments enflamed the situation as hundreds of riot police protected diggers and screaming grannies were dragged away from repossessed ancestral homes.

But the PP pressed on with its programme, building underpasses under Sant Jordi to create a new airport highway, a flyover near Jesús (which has worsened congestion), and a tunnel under the village of Sant Rafel. Minister of Works Stela Matutes expressed the view that though residents publicly voiced opposition to the new roads, privately many were in favour of the scheme, and would be grateful in the future.

This prediction proved inaccurate and her PP party were dismissed from power in the 2007 elections (for only the second time since the 1930s). But with the motorway system virtually completed by the end of the 2007 season, the new highways are here to stay: expect reduced journey times, and a lot more concrete and tarmac.

con and sublimely soft beds and linen. The extensive gardens are also beautifully tended, and the large L-shaped pool is a wonderful place to while away the hours. Breakfast is included; other meals are available on request. €275.

Hostal La Torre

Cap Negret, 2km north of Sant Antoni ☎971 342 271, ⊛www.hostallatorre .com. March–Oct. See map, pp.116–117. Superbly situated above a rocky shelf and with direct sunset views, this relaxed hotel is almost budget boutique. Tidy, simply furnished rooms face a little garden, but the main draw is the magnificent sea-facing terrace area, perfect for drinks and meals. Leading island DJs often drop by to spin a tune or two in the evenings. €65–90.

Pike's

3km east of Sant Antoni ☎971 342 222, ⊛www.pikesibiza.com. See map, pp.94–95. The first rural hotel in Ibiza, *Pike's* was featured in Wham's "Club Tropicana" video, and Freddie Mercury celebrated his birthday here back in the day. The rooms are looking a little dated now, but are very comfortable and have all mod cons. There's also a restaurant, swimming pool and floodlit tennis court. €236–254.

Pensions

Habitaciones Serra

c/de Rossell 13, Sant Antoni ☎971 341 326. May–Oct. See map, pp.110–111. For a cheap bed this is a good deal: a family-run, secure guesthouse in a quiet location close to Sant Antoni's church. All bathrooms are shared. €34.

Hostal Residencia Roig

c/Progress 44, Sant Antoni ☎971 340 483. June–Sept. See map, pp.110–111. This pleasant *hostal* just north of the centre of San An is popular with young British visitors. The 37 attractive rooms have pine furnishings, good-quality beds and private bathrooms, and most have balconies. Guests can use a pool nearby. €56.

Hostal Residencia Salada

c/Soletat 24, Sant Antoni ☎971 341 130. Easter–Oct. See map, pp.110–111. Spick-and-span small hotel, set on a quiet street, with budget singles and doubles, some with private balconies and bathrooms. €40.

Hostal Valencia

c/Valencia 23, Sant Antoni ☎971 341 035, ⓦwww.ibizahostalvalencia.com. See map, pp.110–111. Very well run place that consistently gets good feedback from guests for its service and value for money. Has bright rooms and a pool. €53.

Campsites

Camping Cala Bassa

Cala Bassa ☎971 344 599, ⓦwww .campingcalabassa.com. Beautiful grassy site with plenty of shade close to Cala Bassa beach, with full facilities, including a restaurant. Mobile homes sleeping two to four (€64), caravans (from €35), Bengali bungalows (€65) and hire tents (€5.50) are also available. Regular buses and boats run to and from Sant Antoni in the daytime, but you'll need your own transport or a taxi at night.

Camping Sant Antoni

Ctra Sant Antoni–Ibiza Town, km 1 ☎617 835 845. Pleasant, shady spot, just a five-minute walk from the Egg, though it can get noisy. One-bedroom bungalows are also available (€51 with bathroom, or €32 without), and discounts are available for stays of more than two weeks.

Shops

Amaya

Plaça de s'Església, Sant Antoni. See map, pp.110–111. Funky, inexpensive clothes and a good range of accessories.

Cuatro

c/Ramón i Cayal 4, Sant Antoni. See map, pp.110–111. Hip men's clobber including Stussy and Maharishi, and friendly service.

Kalani

34Q c/del Progrés, Sant Antoni. See map, pp.110–111. Surf specialists with boards for hire, wet suits, clothing and accessories, plus good advice about local conditions.

Terminal

c/Sant Antoni 15, Sant Antoni. See map, pp.110–111. One-stop shop with a good range of vinyl and CDs across most dance genres, plus Internet access and a café.

Restaurants

Can Pujol

c/des Caló, Sant Antoni Bay ☎971 341 407. Daily except Wed 1–3.30pm & 8pm–midnight; closed Dec 1–Jan 6. See map, pp.116–117. Appearances are definitely deceiving: this place close to Port des Torrent may be scruffy, but it's renowned for its seafood. Expect to pay around €40 a head, or more if you pick your victim from the lobster tank.

Casa Thai

Avgda Dr Fleming 34, Sant Antoni ⓣ971 344 038. May–Oct daily 11am–11pm. See map, pp.110–111. The polar opposite of the nearby *Banyan Tree*, this budget Thai offers a Bangkok-style setting, with neon-lit outdoor seating next to a fume-filled highway. Curries, stir-fries and noodle dishes are served up at a furious pace.

El Chiringuito

Cala Gracioneta ⓣ971 348 338. May–Oct daily 12.30–4pm & 8pm–12.30am. See map, pp.116–117. Enjoys a sublime setting right by the water's edge in a sandy cove – it's especially pretty at night, when the restaurant owners float candles in the bay's sheltered waters. The straightforward, moderately priced menu includes fish, paella and delicious barbecued meats, and there's a decent wine list.

El Clodenis

Plaça de s'Església, Sant Rafel ⓣ971 198 545. April–Oct daily 12.30–3.30pm & 8pm–1am. An accomplished, expensive and atmospheric Provençal restaurant with a romantic setting opposite the whitewashed village church – book ahead for a terrace table in summer.

El Rincón de Pepe

c/Sant Mateu, Sant Antoni ⓣ971 340 697. March–Nov 9am–1am. See map, pp.110–111. Your best bet for authentic, inexpensive Spanish grub in central San An. You can either let the staff guide you through the menu, or just tuck into some tapas – leave some room for a local dessert of *flaó* (flan made with mild cheese and mint) or *greixonera* (cake flavoured with cinnamon and lemon – and laced with Cointreau).

Sa Capella

Sant Antoni–Santa Agnès road, km 0.5 ⓣ971 340 057. April–Oct 8pm–1am. See map, pp.116–117. Set in an eighteenth-century chapel just off the Sant Antoni–Santa Agnès road, this is a highly evocative and memorable place for a meal. The expensive Mediterranean menu offers a fairly traditional line-up of meat and fish dishes; all are executed competently enough, though the setting is the real draw here.

Sunset Ashram

Cala Conta ⓣ661 347 222, ⓦwww.sunsetashram.com. May–Oct 10am–2pm. See map, pp.116–117. Looking over idyllic Cala Conta, this stylish new place serves up delicious Spanish and Mediterranean food, juices, smoothies and cocktails. There's a great Balearic vibe, with resident DJs including Jonathan Grey of *Sa Trinxa* fame, and a store selling jewellery and beachwear. Massages can be arranged.

Bars

Bar M

Avgda Dr Fleming, Sant Antoni. May–Oct daily 10am–3am. See map, pp.110–111. In the last few years

▲ BAR M

124

Sant Antoni and around

PLACES

this hip beach bar (owned by
Manumission) has become one
of Ibiza's most celebrated and
popular venues, hosting a series of
gigs by the likes of Babyshambles
and Kasabian. But the venue hit
licensing problems in mid-2007,
and had to shift a number of
concerts to an alternative venue.
Though its future as a live-music
venue is uncertain, *Bar M* is still
well worth a visit as a pre-club
bar, with a huge outdoor terrace
facing the beach and an upper
deck with a bar that functions as
a VIP area for concerts.

Café Mambo

Sunset Strip, Sant Antoni. May–Oct
daily 11am–2am. See map,
pp.110–111. Perhaps Ibiza's key
sunset venue, this bar has a
stylish new outdoor deck and
hosts a glut of events, from
pre-club parties to huge BBC
Radio 1 spectacular. DJs mix up
mellow daytime tunes before
ramping up the house music

Café del Mar

Sunset Strip, Sant Antoni. April–Oct
daily 5pm–1am. See map,
pp.110–111. The bar that first put
Ibiza on the map, the *Café del
Mar* really should be on some
kind of Balearic Beat heritage
trail. Resident DJs maintain José
Padilla's tradition of dreamy
soundscapes, raising the tempo
later with house grooves. Worth
a visit, but sunset pilgrims
beware that the bubblegum-
baroque interior and location
– beneath an unlovely concrete
apartment block – is a letdown.
later in the day.

Coastline

Caló des Moro. April–Oct daily
10am–2am. See map, pp.110–111.
Set beneath a sweeping
Modernist apartment building,
this bar-restaurant has an

extensive sun terrace, pools,
rattan sofas and posh loungers.
There's Spanish food, though
the atmosphere in the restaurant
area can be a little flat.

Kanya

Caló des Moro, Sant Antoni. May–Oct
daily 10am–4am. See map,
pp.116–117. Completely rebuilt
in 2007, this bar has a superb
position right on the coast, a
lovely pool and sunbeds
for daytime chilling. Also
serves snacks.

Kumharas

c/Lugo, Sant Antoni Bay. April–Oct
daily 11am–3am. See map,
pp.116–117. The only bohemian
venue for miles around, this
is an incongruous presence in
concrete packageland. Offers a
radically different take on the
standard sunset-bar formula,
with global beats and ambient
music, plenty of art and
sculpture, a pan-Asian food
menu and regular cultural events.

Savannah

Sunset Strip, Sant Antoni. May–Oct daily
10am–2am. See map, pp.110–111.

▼ FIRE SHOW BY CAFÉ MAMBO

▲ STATUE, KUMHARAS

Long-running bar with an elegant hardwood interior, and a slightly less clubby vibe than some on this strip. The dancefloor action is restricted to the rear backroom bar, which is open till 4am and hosts a plethora of electro-house nights.

The Ship

Plaça de s'Era d'en Manyà. April–Oct daily 10am–3am. See map, pp.110–111. Friendly English-run pub serving British ale, popular with English bar and club workers. It's also a good source of information, with Internet access, plus noticeboards full of apartment rentals and jobs.

Underground

Ibiza Town–Sant Antoni road, km 7 ⓦ www.ibizaunderground.com. April–Oct open selected evenings midnight–4.30am; hosts occasional winter parties. See map pp.94–95. One of Ibiza's least-hyped club-bars, set in a converted farmhouse just north of the main cross-island highway, and yet some of the nights here are exceptional, with the likes of Leftfield's Paul Daley spinning discs. Attracts an older bunch of hip islanders and well-connected international faces, with mainly Spanish-promoted events. The large dancefloor has a potent sound system and there are adjacent lounge-around rooms and a beautiful garden terrace.

Clubs

Amnesia

Ibiza Town–Sant Antoni road, km 5 ⓦ www.amnesia.es. June–Sept. See map, pp.94–95. Musically, *Amnesia* is the most influential club in Ibiza, responsible for igniting the whole British acid-house explosion and the resultant global clubbing revolution. On the right night, it can feel more like a live gig than a nightclub, with an audience of thousands facing the DJ stage in the main room, punching the air to dance anthems under dry-ice-belching cannons.

The vast warehouse-like main room is almost bereft of decor, save a banner or two bearing the promoter's logo, and its huge dancefloor – studded with speaker towers – is ideally

Manumission

The undisputed heavyweight of the Ibiza club scene, Manumission (Latin for "free-dom from slavery") is the biggest night in the island. For over a decade, crowds of 10,000 clubbers descended on *Privilege* to revel in the weekly Manumission experience, enticed by the sheer theatricality and salaciousness of the show, as acrobats, dildo-wielding strippers, lesbian nurses and circus performers created a uniquely Dionysian atmosphere. Following a serious bust-up with *Privilege* in 2007, the whole saucy extravaganza moved to rival club *Amnesia*, and though clubland's greatest spectacle had a new home, it was business as usual.

Manumission is, in effect, two English brothers, Andy and Mike McKay, and their wives Dawn and Claire, whose flair for publicity – including sex-on-stage shows starring Mike and Claire – provoked outrage in the British tabloids and ensured Manumission was one night clubbers could not afford to miss.

Starting out as a Manchester gay night, the Manumission team fled the UK after violent threats from local gangsters. Settling in Ibiza in 1994, the McKays progressed from hosting a party in one bar of the *Ku* club to taking over the entire venue within a few weeks. Manumission packed *Privilege* to the rafters, each season revolving around an innovative theme, the night driven by the imagination and scale of the event, not by the name of the DJ.

In 2004, with dance music suffering a creative downturn, Manumission launched a series of concerts by emerging indie groups. By 2007, the likes of the Arctic Monkeys and Dirty Pretty Things were rocking *Bar M* (see p.123) and other venues near Sant Antoni.

Ibiza Rocks is now very much part of the summer season, though licensing problems at *Bar M* may necessitate a shift to an alternative venue. Manumission is also in need of a good home, and though the move to *Amnesia* worked out well in the 2007 season, there are other options (including the newly enlarged *Space*).

suited to progressive house, trance and techno. Until very recently the terrace occupying the other half of the club was topped by a graceful atrium and beautified by lush greenery, but nowadays only a little sunlight is allowed to penetrate and the terrace has become virtually indistinguishable from the main room – though less intense vocal house tends to be played. Forming an upper level around both sides of the club, the VIP balcony has sofas from where the in-crowd can gaze down on the hoi polloi, though its access, via a rickety metal staircase, is poor.

A lowly farmhouse thirty years ago, *Amnesia* became a hangout for hippies in the 1970s, with music ranging from prog rock to reggae and funk. But after being completely eclipsed by *Ku* in the early 1980s, *Amnesia* reinvented itself as Ibiza's first after-hours club, opening at 5am with eclectic mixes spun by DJ Alfredo. By 1985 *Amnesia* was the most fashionable club on the island with an underground musical policy that encompassed dark minimal proto-house tunes and electro Italian club hits. This spirit of innovation has ensured the club's continuing success, and the owners have proved adept at working with key foreign promoters including Cream, Made in Italy and Sven Vath's Cocoon, while maintaining their own *espuma* (foam) parties. In 2007, Manumission (see p.126) shifted here after a dust-up with *Privilege*, and if Ibiza's most famous club night can be secured on a long-term basis – and there's investment to update the tired-looking internal decor and bathrooms – *Amnesia* looks set for a vibrant future.

Eden

c/Salvador Espiriu, Sant Antoni ⓦwww.edenibiza.com. June–Sept. See map, pp.110–111. *Eden* gives its loyal and mainly British crowd exactly what they want – a raver's delight of pounding house and trance, plenty of club anthems and an orgiastic party atmosphere. Though it's now one of Ibiza's most modern venues, *Eden* was a tacky "niteclub" for years – a disco-throwback that the leading DJs shunned. However, serious investment in 1999 and 2000 resulted in state-of-the-art sound and visual systems, a new industrial-decor refit and multiple new rooms, stages, bars and podiums. BBC Radio One's Dave Pearce and Judge Jules were installed (and remain) resident DJs, and, boosted by massive support from punters, *Eden* assumed local supremacy, and has sustained this success. The club's unpretentiousness means that it's never going to be the most fashionable place on the island, but it can claim to be top dog in San An. Most of the nights here cater to a young audience, but there are also occasional appearances by the likes of veteran DJs Norman Jay and Terry Farley, when purist old-school house is the order of the day.

Eden's exterior is unmissable at night, bristling with electric-blue-lit domes and minarets. Twin steel serpents flank the lobby, while the interior is minimalist in design, with a huge main room under a domed roof; there's a chillout zone and a spacious back room where DJs play more eclectic sounds. A Gaudí-esque steel balcony forms the substantial upper-level gallery, housing a White Room VIP zone, VJ booths and more bars.

Es Paradis

c/Salvador Espiriu, Sant Antoni ⓦwww.esparadis.com. May–Oct. See map, pp.110–111. Aesthetically, *Es Paradis* is undeniably arresting: its square foundation topped by the venue's retractable roof, a beautiful glass pyramid which dominates the skyline of Sant Antoni Bay. The second oldest of the big Ibizan clubs,

▼ EDEN

it celebrated its thirtieth anniversary in 2005. The core crowd here is made up of young British San An–based holidaymakers bent on a great night out – not a particularly cosmopolitan scene, but they sure know how to enjoy themselves.

Inside, though the decor remains immaculately looked after, the disco-era design of neo-Greco columns, marble flooring and verdant foliage is looking dated. Nevertheless, there are ten bars, a giant tropical-fish tank, podium dancers and awesome sound and light systems while, encircling the entire building, the upper balcony contains a second room with alternative sounds.

The club started out as a simple outdoor venue, and grew organically until 1990, when its 120-tonne pyramidal roof proved the most innovative and successful solution to the island's new noise regulations. This set *Es Paradis* up for a consistently successful decade, with water parties (when the whole dancefloor is flooded) and Clockwork Orange club nights ensuring that the place was consistently packed. However, in recent years the club has suffered due to the popularity of the transformed *Eden* over the road, although R&B nights fare well here, and Euro-trance events can also go off.

Privilege

Ibiza Town–Sant Antoni road, km 6 ⓦ www.privilege.es. May–Sept. See map, pp.94–95. Listed in *The Guinness Book of Records* as the world's largest club, *Privilege* was also the Ibiza base of Manumission, the biggest club night on the planet – regularly pulling in 10,000 punters. Then in August 2007, venue and promoter fell out and Manumission decamped to arch-rival *Amnesia*, leaving *Privilege* with a meagre line-up of parties and a huge financial shortfall.

If – and it's a big if, as the club's owners seem incapable of utilizing the venue's massive

▼ PRIVILEGE NIGHTCLUB

potential – you chance upon the right night here it can be an unforgettable experience. As you enter, the sheer scale of the place becomes apparent, with a huge main dancefloor before you, and the DJ plinth above the club's swimming pool. There's a separate Coco Loco zone where DJs spin alternative sounds, and a back room that used to showcase live acts. Fourteen bars are scattered around the club, there are two VIP zones on the upper level, and a vast, metal-framed open-air dome forms the club's alfresco chillout zone. There's even a DJ in the toilets.

Formerly called *Ku*, in the 1980s this was probably the most beautiful, extravagant and luxurious club in Europe. There were huge terraces planted with pine and palm trees, numerous dancefloors and phenomenal sound-and-light systems (the laser shows could be seen in Valencia), a swimming pool and a top-class restaurant. Cocaine spoons and champagne cocktails were *de rigueur*, and there was no shortage of celebrities: Freddie Mercury sang "Barcelona" here with Montserrat Caballé and Grace Jones danced naked in the rain during a thunderstorm. But laws necessitating the construction of a roof

precipitated serious financial problems by the 1990s, and some would say destroyed *Ku*'s unique atmosphere. The club also suffered badly from under-investment. It wasn't until the creative impetous generated by the arrival of Manumission in 1994 that the venue – renamed *Privilege* the following year – started to turn things around. Recent years have had some real highlights, with Manumission and Balearic People filling the venue, but with the former departed, most nights in this vast hangar-like space can be very quiet even in peak season.

Summun

c/Cala de Bou, Sant Antoni Bay. June–Sept. See map, pp.116–117. In Sant Antoni Bay, 3km west of the Egg, *Summun* is a comparatively small (500-capacity) venue, hosting a diverse selection of events, from R&B to Eighties-themed nights. The decor is pretty startling – the walls are painted with swirling images of pastel angels and gods reclining in alpine scenery, plaster-cast gourds and fruit hang from the ceiling, and there are Roman columns and quarry-loads of marble – and entrance and bar prices are reasonable by Ibiza standards.

The south

Southern Ibiza is wildly beautiful and physically diverse, encompassing the island's highest peak, Sa Talaiassa, the shimmering Salines saltpans and drowsy one-horse villages, as well as a craggy coast staked with defence towers. The coastline is lapped by warm, transparent waters and endowed with more than a dozen beautiful beaches. The region has only three resorts – the quiet bays of Cala Vedella and Cala Tarida in the west, and big, brash Platja d'en Bossa in the east; the rest of the shore is more or less pristine. Inland, the rolling, forested countryside is dotted with small, attractive villages. The south is well blessed with dining options, from simple shoreside chiringuitos to swanky country restaurants, as well as a smattering of happening bars.

Sant Josep

Bus #8 from Ibiza Town, Mon–Sat 5 daily, Sun 2 daily; 20min. Bus #8 from Sant Antoni, Mon–Sat 5 daily, Sun 2 daily; 15min. Bus #9 from Sant Antoni, 7 daily. Bus #9 from airport, 6 daily; 15 min. Buses #42 & #26 from Ibiza Town (destination Cala Vedella) May–Oct, 6–9 daily; 20min. Pretty, prosperous and easy-going Sant Josep (San José) has a delightful setting, 200m above sea level in a valley overlooked by the green, forested slopes of Sa Talaiassa. The village itself is of no great size, but it is the main settlement in the region. There's a tidy, trim self-confidence here, best illustrated along the attractive, pint-sized high street, and around the exquisite little central plaza just to the west, where the Moorish-style tiled benches are shaded by pines. From this plaza you have an excellent view across the main road to the imposing, whitewashed **Església de Sant Josep**, dating from 1726. The church has a superb three-storey facade, with a triple-arched porch that extends out from the main body of the building. It's only open for Mass, but if you do get to take a look at the capacious, delightfully cool interior, check out the wooden pulpit, painted with scenes from the life of Christ – a reproduction of the eighteenth-century piece destroyed when the church was gutted in the Spanish Civil War.

▼ SANT JOSEP HIGH STREET

Transport

Getting around the south is easy with your own vehicle, as there's a decent **road network** and plenty of signposts. **Buses** run along the highway between Sant Antoni and Ibiza Town via Sant Josep, and there are also services to some beaches (indicated in the text).

Sant Agustí

About three kilometres north of Sant Josep, the pretty hilltop village of Sant Agustí is so tranquil that all signs of life seem to have been frazzled by the Mediterranean sun. Grouped around the fortified church at the heart of the settlement are a clump of old farmhouses, one of which has been beautifully converted into the *Can Berri Vell* restaurant (see p.144); there's also a village bar, a solitary store and an ancient stone defence tower where the locals once hid from pirates. Captivating views across the hilly interior of the island and down to the southwest coast can be seen from the little plaza next to the landmark **Església de Sant Agustí**, completed in the early nineteenth century. Designed by the Spanish architect Pedro Criollez, this simple rectangular structure has a stark, whitewashed facade, but lacks the frontal porch typical of Ibizan churches.

Sa Talaiassa

Towering above southern Ibiza, the 475-metre peak of Sa Talaiassa is the highest point in the Pitiuses. It's reachable either by an hour-long waymarked hike from Sant Josep, or a dirt road (also signposted) that turns off the road to Cala Carbó, 2km west of Sant Josep. Thickly wooded with aleppo and Italian stone pines, the summit offers exceptional views of southern Ibiza from gaps between the trees. You should easily be able to pick out the humpback cliffs of Jondal and Falcó, the Salines saltpans and plateau-like Formentera – and on very clear days, the mountains of the Dénia peninsula in mainland

▼ ESGLÉSIA DE SANT AGUSTÍ

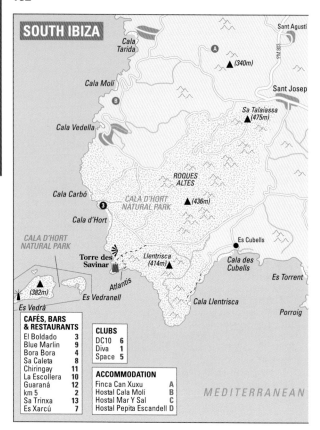

SOUTH IBIZA

Sant Agustí

Cala Tarida

Cala Molí

Sant Josep

Cala Vedella

Sa Talaiassa
▲ (475m)

▲ (340m)

ROQUES
ALTES

Cala Carbó

CALA D'HORT
NATURAL PARK

▲ (436m)

Cala d'Hort

Es Cubells

CALA D'HORT
NATURAL PARK

Torre des
Savinar

Llentrisca
(414m) ▲

Cala des
Cubells

Es Torrent

▲
(382m)

Atlantis

Cala Llentrisca

Es Vedranell

Porroig

Es Vedrà

MEDITERRANEAN

CAFÉS, BARS & RESTAURANTS	
El Boldado	3
Blue Marlin	9
Bora Bora	4
Sa Caleta	8
Chiringay	11
La Escollera	10
Guaraná	12
km 5	2
Sa Trinxa	13
Es Xarcú	7

CLUBS	
DC10	6
Diva	1
Space	5

ACCOMMODATION	
Finca Can Xuxu	A
Hostal Cala Molí	B
Hostal Mar Y Sal	C
Hostal Pepita Escandell	D

Spain, some 50km distant. It's wonderfully peaceful here, the silence broken only by the buzz of cicadas and hum of a number of television antennae. In the 1960s, the summit was the scene of legendary full-moon parties staged by the hippy population.

Cala Tarida

Bus #5 from Sant Antoni, May–Oct 9 daily; Nov–April Thurs only 2 daily; 30min. Bus #38 from Ibiza Town May–Oct 5 daily; 35min. A wide arc of golden sand broken by two small rocky outcrops, Cala Tarida is home to one of Ibiza's more appealing

resorts, a small, family-oriented collection of low-rise hotels surrounding a pretty bay. In high season, the beach gets very busy with German and Spanish holidaymakers, and you'll have to pick your way through rows of umbrellas and sunbeds for a swim. There are plenty of fairly unexciting bars and restaurants to choose from; the best seafood is served at the expensive *Cas Mila*.

Cala Molí

Two kilometres south of Cala Tarida, the serpentine coast road dips down to Cala Molí,

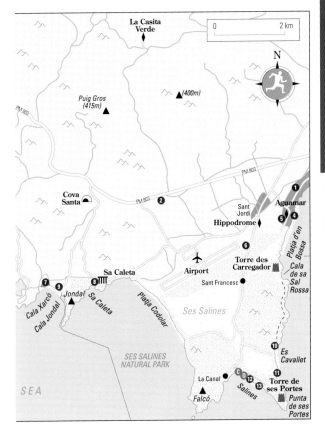

a fine beach at the foot of a seasonal riverbed. Steep cliffs envelop the pebbly cove, which is undeveloped except for the *Restaurante Cala Molí*, an eyesore which sells snacks and has a big swimming pool. The bay's sheltered, deep-green waters are very inviting, and, if you swim across to the cove's southern cliff, you can also explore a small cave. Cala Molí never seems to get too busy, probably because it's not served by buses – if you can get here independently, you'll find it's perfect for a chilled-out day by the sea.

▲ CALA MOLÍ

▲ CALA VEDELLA

Cala Vedella

Buses #26 and #42 from Ibiza Town, May–Oct 6–7 daily; 35–45min.
Continuing south from Cala Molí, the precipitous, shady road twists through the coastal pines for 3km, passing luxury holiday homes before emerging above the long, narrow-mouthed inlet that harbours Cala Vedella. One of Ibiza's most attractive and upmarket resorts, its good-quality villas and well-spaced, low-rise hotels are separated into two main developments around the low hills framing the bay. The sheltered, sandy beach is ideal for families, with calm, very shallow water and a collection of snack bars and restaurants backing onto the sands. DJ José Padilla once owned a bar called *Museum* here – one of the key venues where the Balearic beat mushroomed – but these days there's very little action in Vedella.

Cala Carbó

A tiny, tranquil cove-bay, Cala Carbó, 4km south of Cala Vedella, gets its name from the Catalan word for coal, which was unloaded here until the 1960s. The lovely little sand-and-pebble beach never seems to get too packed and is backed by low sandstone cliffs, and

calm, tempting sea; the mossy, rounded boulders offshore lend the water a deep jade tone. Snorkelling is good off the southern shore up to the rocky point at the mouth of the cove, where colourful wrasse and large schools of mirror fish are common. There are two seafood restaurants at the back of the bay.

Cala d'Hort

Bus #42 from Ibiza Town, May–Oct Mon–Fri 2 daily; 40min. The bus stops on the main road 800m above the beach. Cala d'Hort, 4km south of Cala Carbó, an expansive beach of coarse sand and pebbles, has one of the most spectacular settings in the Balearics. Directly opposite is the startling, vertiginous rock-island of Es Vedrà (see p.135), while the beach is backed by the steep forested hillsides of the Roques Altes peaks, part of the beautiful **Cala d'Hort Natural Park**. There's a wonderfully isolated feel here, and the remote location, wedged into Ibiza's southwest corner, ensures that things never get too busy.

You'll find three good fish restaurants by the shore – the best is *Es Boldado* on the northern lip of the bay (see p.144). If you're smitten by the beauty of the scene and want to hang around a while, try asking at the *El Carmen* restaurant, which has inexpensive rooms for rent.

Es Vedrà

Rising from the sea like the craggy crest of a semi-submerged volcano, the limestone outcrop of Es Vedrà is one of the most startling sights in the western Mediterranean. Despite its height (378m), it is only visible once you get within a few kilometres of Cala d'Hort. Legends surround the much-photographed rock, and it's said to be the island of the sirens (the sea nymphs who tried to lure Odysseus from his ship in Homer's epic), as well as the holy isle of the Carthaginian love and fertility goddess, Tanit. A reclusive Carmelite priest, Father Palau i Quer, reported seeing visions of the Virgin Mary and satanic rituals here in the nineteenth century. Sailors and scuba divers have told of compasses swinging wildly and gauges malfunctioning as they approach the island, and there have been innumerable stories of UFO sightings.

These days, Es Vedrà is inhabited only by wild goats, a unique subspecies of the Ibizan wall lizard and a small colony of the endangered Eleanor's falcon. You can get to the island from Cala d'Hort by renting a four-metre boat, which will carry four, from Bruno's hut (☎607 147 155; €60 per hour) behind the beach; as the boat's engine has just 10HP a skipper's licence is not necessary. Vedrà has no beaches, however, and there's little to see, bar scrub bush and a lizard or two – even the goats usually prove elusive.

Torre des Savinar and Atlantis

Two kilometres along the exhilaratingly scenic road from Cala d'Hort to Es Cubells, a right-hand turn-off leads to Torre des Savinar, a defence tower built in 1763 – it's also known (and should be signposted) as Torre d'en Pirata. The dirt track ends after 500m, where there's a small roundabout and parking area. From here it's a ten-minute walk to the coastal cliffs, where there's an amazing

▼ ES VEDRANELL AND ES VEDRÀ

view over the sea to Es Vedrà, particularly at sunset.

From the tower itself there are even better vistas over Vedrà's sister island **Es Vedranell**, which resembles a sleeping dragon, its snout and spiky backbone protruding from the water.

Directly below the Torre des Savinar you can make out the outline of **Atlantis**, an ancient shoreside quarry some 200m down. To get there, retrace your steps to the parking area and take another path that sets off to the right (east); you'll quickly reach the clifftop trailhead, from where Atlantis is a thirty-minute hike away. The very steep, well-trodden path is easy to follow; it flattens out after fifteen minutes beside a small **cave**, where there's a beautiful etched image of a Buddha, said to have been drawn by a Japanese traveller. From the cave, you have to plough your way through sand dunes, but as you near the shore, the hewn forms of the ancient quarry – set at oblique angles from the bedrock – become clear. The stone here was used in the construction of Ibiza Town's magnificent walls.

Between the rock outcrops, shimmering indigo- and emerald-tinged pools of trapped seawater add an ethereal dimension to the scene. Much of the stone has been carved by hippies with mystic imagery – blunt-nosed faces resembling Maya gods, swirling abstract doodles and graffiti – while blocks of stone hang suspended by wires from the rock face. At the edge of the promontory there's a wonderful, partly painted carving of a Cleopatra-like oriental queen. Bring, plenty of water and sun cream, as there's no shade.

Es Cubells

Bus #42 from Ibiza Town, May–Oct Mon–Fri 2 daily; 30min. South of Sant Josep, a signposted road weaves around the eastern flank of Sa Talaiassa, past terraces of orange and olive trees, to the southern coast and the tiny cliffside village of Es Cubells. The settlement owes its place on the map to Father Palau i Quer, a Carmelite priest who saw visions of the Virgin Mary on nearby Es Vedrà in the 1850s, and who persuaded the Vatican to construct a chapel here in 1855 for the local farmers and fishermen. Magnificently positioned above the Mediterranean, the simple whitewashed sandstone church is the focal point of the hamlet. Adjoining the church, *Bar Llumbi* is an inexpensive bar-restaurant (May–Oct, closed Mon) ideal for a *bocadillo* and a *copa* with a view.

Cala des Cubells

Signposted from Es Cubells' church, the minuscule Cala des Cubells beach lies 1km from the village, via a couple of hairpin turns. It's one of Ibiza's least-visited spots, consisting of a slender strip of grey, tide-polished stones with a few sunbeds and umbrellas and a somewhat overpriced restaurant, *Ses Boques*. If you're looking for an isolated place to get an all-over tan, head to the left past a strip of fishing huts, where three tiny, untouched stony beaches lie below grey, crumbling cliffs.

Cala Llentrisca

Southwest of Es Cubells, the road hugs the eastern slopes of the Llentrisca headland, descending for 3km past luxurious modern villas towards

▲ CALA LLENTRISCA

the lovely, unspoilt cove of Cala
Llentrisca, cut off from the rest
of the island by soaring pine-
clad slopes. You'll need your
own transport to get here; park
beside the final villa at the end
of the road and walk the last ten
minutes along a rugged path.
Bear in mind that there's very
little shade, and nothing on the
pebbly shoreline except a row of
seldom-used fishing huts and a
lot of compressed seaweed, with
a yacht or two often moored in
the translucent waters.

Es Torrent

A small, sandy cove beach at
the foot of a dry riverbed, Es
Torrent lies 7km south of Sant
Josep. To get here, take the road
to Es Cubells, and follow the
signposted turn-off that winds
down towards the Porroig
promontory. Es Torrent's waters
are shallow and invitingly
turquoise, and offer decent
snorkelling around the cliffs at
the edge of the bay. Though
the beach is lovely, many
people come here just for the
expensive seafood restaurant,
Es Torrent.

Cala Xarcó

From Es Torrent, having
looped around the Porroig
peninsula, dotted with luxury
villas, you can follow a dirt
track that continues northeast
for 400m to Cala Xarcó, a
quiet strip of sand that only
Ibizans and the odd yachtie
seem to have stumbled upon.
The coastal sabina pines here
offer a little shade. There's also
a sunbed or two for rent, and
the superb, but very pricey,
Restaurant Es Xarcú (see p.145),
which specializes in seafood.

Cala Jondal

The broad pebble beach of
Cala Jondal lies between the
promontories of Porroig and
Jondal some 9km southeast of
Sant Josep. A stony seashore
at the base of terraces planted
with fruit trees, Jondal's
kilometre-long strip of smooth
rounded stones and patches
of imported sand doesn't
make one of the island's finest
swimming spots, but there's
always some space here and
you should have no problem
getting a sunbed and shade.
There are some good beachside
restaurants including *Yemaná*
and *Tropicana* (which also serves
excellent fresh fruit juices). On
the east side, the celeb-geared
Blue Marlin is a spectacular
beach restaurant-cum-bar-
cum-club which offers some
of the island's most expensive
cocktails and most elegant
sun loungers. There's also a

▲ BLUE MARLIN, CALA JONDAL

massage tent (€25 per hour), located close to the centre of the beach. If you're coming from Xarcó, Cala Jondal is a couple of minutes' scramble over the cliff behind *Restaurant Es Xarcú*; you can also drive via a precipitous dirt road from the beach – after 200m, take the first right beside some walled villas.

Sa Caleta

Bus #26 from Ibiza Town, May–Oct 6 daily; 25min. Four kilometres around the coast from Cala Jondal lie the **ruins** of Sa Caleta, the first Phoenician settlement in Ibiza. Established around 650 BC on a low promontory beside a tiny natural harbour, the small site was only occupied for about fifty years, before the Phoenicians moved to the site of what is now Ibiza Town. Today, a high metal fence surrounds the foundations of the village, once home to several hundred people, who lived by fishing, hunting and farming

wheat as well as smelting iron for tools and weapons. The ruins are visually unimpressive, but the site is a peaceful place to visit, with expansive views over an azure sea towards Platja Codolar and Cap des Falcó.

Just west of the site are Sa Caleta's **beaches**, three tiny adjoining bays sometimes labelled as "Bol Nou" on maps. The first bay, a hundred-metre strip of coarse golden sand, is the busiest spot, and very popular with Ibizan families at weekends – there are some sunbeds and umbrellas to rent here in summer, excellent swimming and snorkelling, and the well-regarded *Restaurante Sa Caleta* (see p.145). The other two bays, both secluded and pebbly, are to the west of the sandy bay, via a path that winds along the shore below Sa Caleta's low sandstone cliffs. For a superb Thai massage check out the excellent Tree House Body Shop (from €25) behind the beach.

Platja Codolar

East of Sa Caleta, a road runs parallel to the ochre-coloured coastal cliffs, heading towards the airport and Sant Jordi. One kilometre along, there's a turn-off for Platja Codolar, a sweeping pebble beach that stretches for over 3km southeast, running close to the airport runway and skirting the fringes of the Salines saltpans. Even at the height of summer, there are rarely more than a dozen or so (mainly nude) swimmers and sunbathers here, and the place would be very peaceful were it not for the regular interruption of jet engines revving up on the runway or screaming overhead. It's also possible to get to the opposite end of Platja Codolar via the main road to Salines beach; turn off at km 3.6 and follow the signposts for the *Cap des Falcó* restaurant.

La Casita Verde

11km northwest of Sant Josep ☎971 187 353, ⓦ www.greenheart.info. Enjoying a wonderful location in a remote valley between Sant Josep and Sant Rafel, La Casita Verde is a model ecology centre demonstrating low-impact living in a fun and educational way. Electricity is mostly generated by solar and wind power and water-saving and recycling techniques are fundamental to the project. There's plenty to investigate, including structures made from bottles and cans, and fields of aloe vera and carob trees (used for flavouring drinks and cakes). La Casita Verde is run by volunteers and is open each Sunday for visitors wishing to learn more about sustainable lifestyle techniques. For directions,

opening times and details of special events check out their website.

Sant Jordi

Buses #9, #10, #11, #24, #26 & #42 from Ibiza Town 26–44 daily; 15min. Trapped in a suburban no-man's-land between Ibiza Town and the beaches to the south, Sant Jordi is a pretty nondescript place, though the area's once-notorious traffic congestion has been alleviated by a series of ugly new underpasses and flyovers. The main point of interest is the **Església de Sant Jordi**, Ibiza's most fortress-like church, just east of the centre. With mighty angled walls gashed with embrasures and topped with full battlements – all security measures to keep out pirates – it's well worth a visit. Inside, the austerity of the gingham-tiled floor and simple wooden benches seem at odds with the gaudy modern altarpiece, installed in 1990.

The only other reason to visit Sant Jordi is for the very popular Saturday **market** (9am–2pm), actually more of a car boot sale, held in the dustbowl of the **hippodrome**, a former horse-and-buggy race track. It's Ibiza's most quirky affair, far less commercialized than the hippy markets, with a good selection of junk jewellery, trashy clothes, secondhand books and furniture.

Platja d'en Bossa

Bus #14 from Ibiza Town, May–Oct every 30min, plus hourly nightbuses; Nov–April hourly; 15min. A kilometre east of Sant Jordi, and merging into Figueretes to the north (see p.64), the conventional, Costa-style resort of Platja d'en Bossa is

Platja d'en Bossa hike

It's possible to hike from Platja d'en Bossa to Es Cavallet along an easy-to-follow shady path that trails the coastline, passing rocky coves and pine forests. From the extreme southernmost part of Platja d'en Bossa beach head to the sixteenth-century **Torre des Carregador**, a defence tower just above the beach, and continue to the south. The hike takes about an hour and a half and doesn't stray more than 50m or so from the sea. There are no refreshments along the way.

stretched out along the island's longest beach – a ruler-straight, three-kilometre-long strip of wonderfully fine, pale sand. Lining the beach are a gap-toothed row of hotel blocks, many abruptly thrown up in the later Franco years and others still in various stages of construction; behind these lies a secondary strip of cafés, touristy restaurants, German *bierkellers*, British pubs, car-rental outlets and minimarkets filled with plastic dolphins, perfume, cigarettes and sun cream. Though Platja d'en Bossa is predominantly a family resort, it's also famous for the messy antics at beachside club-bar *Bora Bora* (see p.145) and the legendary king of clubs, *Space* (see p.147).

Despite the tourist tat, Platja d'en Bossa is increasingly popular as a base for savvy older clubbers who have tired of the San An scene and stay here to take advantage of the location – a few kilometres from both Ibiza Town and the sands at Salines. Its main drawback is the lack of decent restaurants, most of which serve bland "international" fare.

Aguamar

May–Oct 10am–6pm. €18, children over 2 years €9. Bus #14 from Ibiza Town, every 30min; 15min. With a great selection of slides and a vast central swimming-pool area suitable for all ages, this water park is a lot of fun. It's also well managed, with attendants on standby to ensure safety requirements are enforced. It does get very busy in July and August, when you'll have to queue for a while for the best rides (which include the "Black Hole" and "Super Toboggan"). There are several snack bars and picnic areas, though you have to pay extra to use sunbeds and lockers.

▼ ES CAVALLET

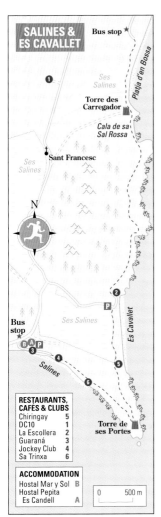

close to *La Escollera* restaurant (see p.144) and the car park, attracts a mixed bunch of families and couples, but the southern half of the beach – the nicest stretch – is almost exclusively gay, centred around the superb *Chiringay* bar-café (see p.143).

Salines beach

Bus #11 from Ibiza Town, May–Oct 10–12 daily; Nov–April 2 daily; 25min. A beautiful kilometre-long strip of powdery, pale sand backed by pines and dunes, Salines beach is Ibiza's most fashionable place to pose. In the height of summer the sands here are thick with celebs and Spanish footballers, with sunbeds and tables reserved days in advance. The beach is interspersed with rocky patches, and bars dot the shoreline, which changes steadily from a family-friendly environment close to the *Guaraná* café in the north into the island's premier navel-gazing spot around the über-hip *Sa Trinxa* café in the south, where you can sunbathe nude.

Beyond *Sa Trinxa* are a succession of tiny sandy coves, enveloped by unusual rock formations – some were quarried centuries ago, while more recently, talented sculptors have carved images into the coastal stone, including a Medusa-like figure and a fang-baring dragon wearing a Mayan-style headdress. These mini-beaches tend to get grabbed fairly early in the day and jealously guarded as private bays by dedicated – and pretty territorial – sunbathers. Beyond the coves, the sands give way to a slender rocky

Es Cavallet

Franco's Guardia Civil fought a futile battle against nudism on this stunning beach for years, arresting hundreds of naked hippies before the kilometre-long stretch of sand was finally designated Ibiza's first naturist shore in 1978. The northern end of the beach,

▲ SALINES BEACH

Above the swirling currents and a handful of surf-battered fishing huts is a two-storey, sixteenth-century defence tower, **Torre de ses Portes**, which commands superb views of the chain of tiny islands that reach out to Formentera. One of these, Illa des Penjats (Island of the Hanged), was used for executions until the early twentieth century; another, Illa des Porcs (Pig Island), was once a pig-smugglers' stronghold. Both islands are topped by the lighthouses that guide ships and ferries through the treacherous Es Freus channel between Ibiza and Formentera.

promontory, topped at its end by the **Torre de ses Portes** defence tower.

Punta de ses Portes

A fifteen-minute walk south from Es Cavallet beach is Ibiza's most southerly point, Punta de ses Portes, a lonely, rocky spot, often lashed by winds and waves.

Hotels

Finca Can Xuxu

4km west of Sant Josep ☎971 801 584, ⓦwww.canxuxu.com. April–Oct. Fine new rural hotel, owned by an English-speaking Frenchman, that has glimpses of Ibiza's west coast and the offshore islet of Conillera from its grounds. All accommodation

Salines saltpans

Ibiza's spectacular saltpans, which stretch across 435 hectares in the south of the island, were its only reliable source of wealth for more than 2000 years. The Phoenicians first developed the land and, although Roman, Vandal and Visigoth invaders continued to maintain the saltpans, it was the Moors, experts at hydraulic technology, who developed the system of sluice gates, mini-windmills and water channels that's still in use today. Each May approximately 2500 cubic metres of seawater is left to evaporate, forming a ten-centimetre crust of pinky-white powder that is scooped up and amassed in huge salt hills. Around 50,000 tonnes of salt are exported annually (down from 70,000 a few years ago); the finest quality is shipped to Denmark and Norway for salting cod, and the rest to Scotland for salting roads in winter. The pans are part of a wetland reserve and are an important habitat for **birds**. Storks, herons and flamingoes stop to rest and refuel at what is one of the first points of call on the migratory route from Africa, while over 200 species are in permanent residence, from the osprey and black-necked grebe to the Kentish plover. A visitor centre has long been planned next to the church in Sant Francesc, but until it opens you're best viewing the pans at sunset from the Sant Jordi–La Canal road, around the km 3 marker; beware clouds of mosquitoes at dusk and dawn, especially in September.

is in converted outbuildings set to the side of the main house, and the communal area has comfy sofas and a TV/DVD for guests' use. The spacious rooms are rustic-chic, with traditional features and Egyptian-cotton bed linen; two have private sun terraces. To the rear of the hotel you'll find a large pool, in a magnificent garden bursting with tropical plants.

Hostal Cala Molí

1km south of Cala Molí ☏ 971 806 002, ⓦ www.calamoli.com. May–Oct. High in the hills with great sunset views, this small, welcoming hotel has attractive, good-value accommodation decorated with textile wall-hangings; all rooms overlook the sea and some come with their own lounge (€100–118). There's a small pool, a restaurant, and breakfast is included. €85–100.

Hotel Los Jardins de Palerm

Sant Josep ☏ 971 800 318, ⓦ www .jardinsdepalerm.com. A very tastefully decorated luxury hotel, a few minutes' walk away from the village of Sant Josep. The rooms have been given a minimalist makeover and exude contemporary style. Two pools enjoy a lush garden setting, and you'll find numerous sun terraces. A continental breakfast is included, though there's little in the way of service at other times. €220–253.

Pensions

Hostal Mar y Sal

Salines beach ☏ 971 396 584. For beach-lovers on a budget this basic *hostal*, just

behind Salines beach, is ideal. The smallish rooms have private showers and some have balconies with views of the sand dunes; there's also a good bar/restaurant downstairs. €46.

Hostal Pepita Escandell

Salines beach ☏ 971 396 583. May–Oct. A simple but very friendly place at the northern end of Salines beach where the rooms are spartan but clean; some have private bathrooms. There's a communal kitchen and a tranquil garden. €43.

Cafés

Chiringay

Es Cavallet beach ⓦ www.chiringay .com. April–Oct daily 10am–8pm. Fine beachfront bar-restaurant on Ibiza's main gay beach with a healthy Mediterranean menu that encompasses seafood and grilled meats. It's renowned for its fruit juices and smoothies, and the decked terrace is the perfect spot to share a bottle of cava.

Sa Trinxa

Salines beach ⓦ www.satrinxa .com. Daily: April–Oct 11am–10pm; Nov–March 11am–7pm. The

▼ SA TRINXA

definitive Ibizan *chiringuito*, set at the southern end of the hippest beach on the island. Outstanding, eclectic mixes courtesy of resident DJ Jonathan Grey and guests are beamed out to the assorted supine Balearic wildlife: club faces, models and wannabes, party freaks and Euro slackers. Meals are served, but the *bocadillos* are some of the priciest in Ibiza.

Restaurants

Es Boldado

Cala d'Hort ☎ 626 494 537 (mobile). Daily 1–4pm & 7.30–10.30pm. Overlooking Es Vedrà, this seafood restaurant boasts a stunning location, particularly at sunset. The menu offers superb paella (€27 for two), *arroz marinera* and plenty of excellent grilled fish (from €14). Portions are huge, though there's nothing for dessert except ice cream. You can drive to *Es Boldado* via a signposted side road just northwest of Cala d'Hort, or it's a five-minute walk west of the same beach, past the fishermen's huts.

Can Berri Vell

Plaça Major, Sant Agustí ☎ 971 344 321, ⊛ www.canberrivell.com. June–Sept daily 8pm–midnight; April, May & Oct closed Sun. The setting is the real draw at this village restaurant – eat inside a seventeenth-century Ibizan *casament* (farmhouse) or on the large dining terrace which borders the village church. The menu has got a lot fancier in recent years, but the grilled meats work best. Expect to pay about €30 per person including drinks.

El Destino

c/Atalaya 15, Sant Josep ☎ 971 800 341. Mon–Sat 7.30pm–midnight. This fine, intimate place is famous for its tapas, which are inventively prepared and inexpensively priced, with plenty of choice for vegetarians. There's a small pavement terrace and a comfortable dining room. Book ahead on summer nights.

La Escollera

Es Cavallet beach ☎ 971 396 572. May–Oct daily 1pm–12.30am; Nov–April 1–5.30pm. Highly enjoyable restaurant, with sweeping views

▼ CAN BERRI VELL

▲ BORA BORA

of Es Cavallet beach and across to Formentera. There's a huge outdoor terrace by the sea and a capacious interior (with a fireplace for the winter months). Majors in seafood, including *zarzuela* (fish and seafood casserole) and grilled dorado, though there are other options including couscous and country-style chicken. Expect to pay around €30 a head.

Sa Caleta

Sa Caleta beach ☎ 971 187 095. May–Oct noon–midnight; Nov–April noon–7pm. Fine, fairly expensive seafood restaurant, just behind this popular cove. Fish is grilled, baked or served in *salsa verde*; there's also good paella and great apple tart. For a memorable finish, order the house special, Sa Caleta coffee, which is prepared at your table and includes a generous dose of brandy and lemon and orange peel.

Es Xarcú

Cala Xarcó ☎ 971 187 867. April–Oct daily 1–11pm. Like many seafood restaurants in Ibiza, this beachside place looks very humble, with rickety tables and chairs, but the quality of the cooking, freshness of the fish and size of the bill defy appearances. The signature dish here is *pez de San Pedro* (John

Dory), which is cooked in a butter-rich white-wine sauce. It's not an easy place to find, but best approached from Es Torrent – the yachts offshore are a giveaway that most diners arrive by boat.

Bars

Bar Can Bernat Vinya

Sant Josep. Daily 7am–midnight. Unpretentious locals' local in Sant Josep village, serving inexpensive tapas and snacks, where Spanish is a second language to Eivissenc. In summer, tables spill onto the delightful plaza outside; the conversation usually centres on hunting and the strange ways of *giris* (tourists).

Bora Bora

Platja d'en Bossa. May–Sept daily noon–4am. Bombastic beachside bar-club that dishes up pounding beats to an army of young swimwear-clad ravers. The authorities do periodically call a halt to the party (which can get pretty messy, with pilled-up punters gurning in the sunshine) but as there's no entrance charge and (fairly) reasonably priced drinks, this place can draw a cast of thousands on some August nights.

km 5

Ibiza Town–Sant Josep road, km 5.6. June–Sept daily 9pm–4am; Oct–May Wed, Fri & Sat 11pm–4am. Urbane "lounge garden" that draws an international crowd, set in a rustic nowhereland west of Ibiza Town, with Moroccan tents and rugs for relaxed drinking and socializing. Drinks are pricey, but there's an outstanding cocktail list (try the Amaretto sours) and the ambience is worth it, with a very cosmopolitan, relaxed vibe. The (pricey) restaurant here seems to get better every year, with delicious fish, free-range chicken and a good vegetarian selection. DJs often spin tunes late on, though Ibiza's draconian licensing laws mean that the dancefloor area is periodically roped off.

Racó Verd

Plaça de l'Església, Sant Josep ⓦwww.racoverd.es. May–Oct Mon–Sat 10am–2am; Nov–April Mon–Sat 10am–8pm, until late for special events. Highly enjoyable and popular village bar with a great central terrace set around an ancient olive tree. Famous for its fresh juices, but a full breakfast menu is also offered, as well as tapas and substantial Med and Spanish dishes. Hosts an eclectic selection of live-music nights in summer – jazz, flamenco, rock and blues, acoustic, African, Latin and sitar – and also offers winter events including films, gigs and *cuentocuentas*

(storytelling) nights. There's Wi-Fi Internet access here too.

Clubs

DC10

Sant Jordi–Salines road, km 1. June–Oct. One of *the* success stories of the last decade, this scruffy club has a raw, unpretentious appeal that's completely different to the more corporate-minded venues. Forgoing commerce for pure party spirit, the atmosphere here can rival old acid-house times on the right day, as a euphoric international crowd dance in the sunshine. It can be a very hardcore experience however, with many clubbers getting thoroughly wasted (perhaps due to the widespread use of ketamine).

Anglo-Italian Circo Loco ensemble started a Monday

▼ DC10

▲ SPACE

daytime slot here in 2000, which was followed by some amazing sessions, including epic performances by Danny Tenaglia and Timo Maas. This Monday session (beginning at 8am and winding down in the early evening) is the one to try and catch, though *DC10* offers some night-time club action too.

The venue is located in a rural corner of Ibiza, a stone's throw from the airport. The covered terrace, where all the action takes place, is little more than a wall around a paved floor, topped by an ugly roof, and bordered by the giant reeds of neighbouring fields. Adjoining the terrace is a spartan back room, with harder, more progressive sounds, that rarely gets busy.

Diva

Platja d'en Bossa. June–Sept. This 800-capacity club opened for a few weeks in the 2007 season, but owners *Eden* closed the doors after failing to attract sufficient paying punters. Formerly the tacky *Kiss discoteca*, the haunt of wet T-shirt competitions and sing-a-long holiday hits, it later metamorphosed into the stylish, but ultimately unconvincing *Sonny* and could yet re-emerge as a serious venue in the future.

Space

Platja d'en Bossa ⓦ www.space -ibiza.es. June–Oct. Twice voted "the best club in the world" at the International Dance Music Awards, *Space* has been revamped in the last few years from an average venue with a unique asset (its legendary open-air terrace) into what must now rank as the island's best club. The transformation has been near total, involving the construction of a glass roof over the old terrace, the building of a huge additional Sunset Terrace, a Salon area and the gutting and renovation of the vast, dark main room (which becomes the prime focus of the club when headlining DJs bring the party action to a close). The new upper level has a superb open-air chillout terrace that wraps around the front of this vast temple of dance, an adjoining alternative room called the Caja Roja (Red Box) and a separate VIP zone for good measure. For opening and closing parties, even these huge spaces are deemed insufficient, and the club expands out into a neighbouring car park – when upwards of 10,000 clubbers can be accommodated.

Space started life back in 1989 as a conference centre and disco, gaining credibility in the early 1990s by kicking off after sunrise when the main clubs were closing. A carry-on-clubbing scene centred on the venue's open-air terrace cemented *Space* as perhaps Europe's most exciting DJ venue, attracting a very cosmopolitan crowd of Balearic-based scenesters, international party people and a big gay contingent. Strict noise regulations necessitated the building of a roof over the terrace in 2005, and the venue's owners have responded by creating a series of arenas, and a less claustrophobic feel, even if the magic of grooving in the sunshine has been lost.

Space now hosts more DJs and parties than any other club in Ibiza, with gay meganight La Troya enticed from *Amnesia* in 2007, Carl Cox setting up a summer residency and Sunday's We Love still the mother of all club sessions, with a roster of over 20 DJs, beginning at 8am and finishing at 6am. Expect more double-headers in the future, as it's now possible for the owners to divide the club into two halves, and book separate promoters for each section. And *Space*'s opening and closing parties still unquestionably define the parameters of Ibiza's clubbing season – when *Space* closes in early October, that's all folks. Until next summer, of course.

Formentera

Tranquil, easy-going Formentera could hardly be more of a contrast to Ibiza. The island is very flat, consisting of two shelf-like plateaux connected by a narrow central isthmus, and has a population of just 7000. Most visitors are drawn here by the languid pace of life, as well as some of the longest, whitest, cleanest and least crowded beaches in Spain, surrounded by exceptionally clear water. This unhurried appeal belies a troubled past: the struggle of eking out a living from the saltpans and sun-baked soil, combined with outbreaks of the plague and attacks by pirates, led Formentera to be completely abandoned in the late fourteenth century, only to be resettled in 1697. The island has just one resort, Es Pujols, a restrained, small-scale affair, with the pick of the beaches close by. Inland, the beautiful, arid countryside is a patchwork of golden wheatfields, vines, carob and fig trees, divided by old dry-stone walls. Of the three villages, the central, diminutive capital, Sant Francesc Xavier, is the most interesting, while the island's extremes – where you'll find lonely lighthouses and stunning coastal scenery – are captivating.

La Savina

Set in a small natural harbour in the northwest corner of the island, orderly La Savina is likely to be your first view of Formentera, as all ferries from Ibiza dock here. Never more than a minor settlement for the export of salt and planks of sabina pine (from which it takes its name), it's still a sleepy place today, ferry traffic aside. While not that absorbing, the modern harbour is pleasant enough, and the souvenir shops and cafés are perfectly placed if you need to while away an hour or so before your ferry departs.

Es Campament

On the eastern edge of La Savina, just south of the highway, the concentration

▼ MARINA, LA SAVINA

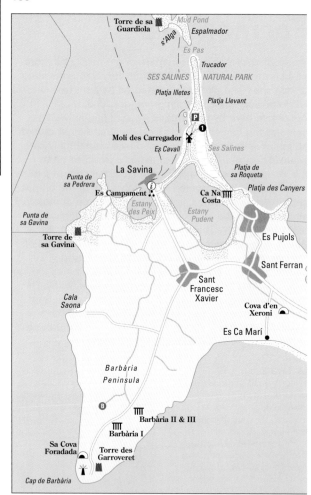

Torre de sa Guardiola
Mud Pond
s'Alga
Espalmador
Es Pas
Trucador
SES SALINES NATURAL PARK
Platja Illetes
Platja Llevant
Molí des Carregador
Es Cavall
Ses Salines
La Savina
Platja de sa Roqueta
Punta de sa Pedrera
Platja des Canyers
Es Campament
Ca Na Costa
Estany des Peix
Estany Pudent
Punta de sa Gavina
Es Pujols
Torre de sa Gavina
Sant Ferran
Cala Saona
Sant Francesc Xavier
Cova d'en Xeroni
Es Ca Marí
Barbària Peninsula
Barbària II & III
Barbària I
Sa Cova Foradada
Torre des Garroveret
Cap de Barbària

Transport

Most visitors choose to get around Formentera independently, and renting transport is easy (see p.171). There's a good network of Green Route **cycle paths** (leaflets are available from the tourist office, see p.152; for bike rental see p.172). The island also has a pretty reasonable **bus network**, with daily services operating a loop around the main settlements of La Savina, Es Pujols, Sant Ferran and Sant Francesc every two hours or so between May and October, plus buses to La Mola and Platja Illetes. Services are much reduced for the rest of the year.

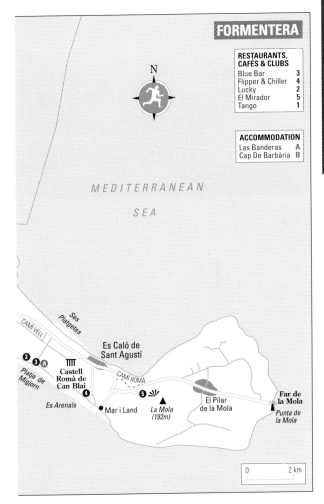

FORMENTERA

RESTAURANTS, CAFÉS & CLUBS

Blue Bar	3
Flipper & Chiller	4
Lucky	2
El Mirador	5
Tango	1

ACCOMMODATION

Las Banderas	A
Cap De Barbària	B

MEDITERRANEAN SEA

camp of Es Campament housed several hundred prisoners-of-war and anti-Francoists in the years following the Spanish Civil War. Very little remains today, except some walls entwined with barbed wire, a ruined meeting hall and a plaque bearing a poem in Catalan by local writer Joan Puig, but an eerie presence still lingers.

Estany Pudent and Estany des Peix

Buses on the La Savina–La Mola highway pass within 300m of both lakes. Heading southeast out of La Savina, the island's main highway passes a sprawl of roadside warehouses that almost obscures Formentera's two **salt lakes**, the island's main wetland habitats. On the left, Estany Pudent, or "Stinking Pond", is

▲ ESTANY PUDENT

the larger of the two, an oval expanse that smells better now an irrigation channel has been opened to allow sea water in, though a rotten aroma sometimes hangs in the air on still days. Ringed by scrub bush and an unsightly jumble of bungalows, it's not exactly pretty, but is popular amongst birdwatchers, who come to see herons and egret, black-necked grebe, warbler and even the odd flamingo. Dirt tracks run around the entire lake; you can get to the shoreline via a left-hand turn-off 500m along the main highway from La Savina, which passes through a small patch of saltpans.

Smaller Estany des Peix, to the right of the highway via a turn-off 1km south of La Savina, has a narrow mouth to the sea, and its shallow waters act as an ideal nursery for young fish. The brackish lagoon is no more picturesque than its neighbour, and not as rich birding territory, but there are plenty of terns and ducks and you may encounter the odd wader. Endemic marine organisms found in the lake have also been found to have strong cancer-fighting qualities. After years of successful clinical trials in the USA and several EU countries, an extract from a tunicate found in Estany des Peix is to be marketed as

Arrival and information

Several companies run **ferries** and **hydrofoils** between Ibiza Town and La Savina (July–Sept 13–17 daily; Nov–March 5 daily; April–June & Oct 8–14 daily; 30–65min; €22–37 return). In addition, boat operators in most Ibiza resorts offer **day-trips** to Formentera.

Just behind the harbour in La Savina, Formentera's only **tourist information** office (Mon–Fri 10am–2pm & 5–7pm, Sat 10am–2pm; ☎971 322 057, ⓦwww.formentera.es) has a good stock of glossy leaflets covering the island's history, environment, hotels, beaches and Green Routes, and the staff are extremely helpful. For accommodation information, head next door to the Central de Reservas Formentera office (☎971 323 224, ⓦwww.formenterareservations.com), which has an extensive list of apartments and houses for rent.

Yondelis (ET-743), a treatment for tumours.

Sant Francesc Xavier

Bus from La Savina, May–Oct 15 daily; Nov–April 3 daily; 5min.
Formentera's tiny capital, Sant Francesc Xavier, 2km southeast of La Savina, is a quiet little town with an attractive network of pretty, whitewashed streets. It's not much of a social centre – though it does have a few bars – and Sant Francesc's residents have the reputation of being a somewhat sedate bunch. If you've arrived from the mainland or from Ibiza Town, you'll have to get used to very un-Spanish timekeeping here – eating before 10pm and drinking up shortly after 11pm.

Plaça de sa Constitució

The heart of Sant Francesc is the Plaça de sa Constitució, a fetching little square with a few benches scattered between gnarled olive trunks and sickly-looking palm trees. Consecrated in 1726, the forbidding, fortified **Església de Sant Francesc Xavier** stands

▼ ESGLÉSIA DE SANT FRANCESC XAVIER

on the north side of the plaza, its stark plastered facade embellished only with a tiny window set high in the wall. Until the mid-nineteenth century cannons were mounted on the building's flat roof as an extra line of defence against the ever-present threat of pirate attacks. Entering the church through the mighty main doors, strengthened with iron panelling, the sombre interior has a single barrel-vaulted nave, five tiny side-chapels and a gaudy gold-plated altar. Beside the doorway, the large, alabaster baptismal font is its most curious feature, decorated with a crudely executed ox's head and weathered human faces. It's thought to date from Vandal times, but no one is quite sure who originally brought it here. Adjoining the church to the south is the unpretentious, blue-shuttered old government building, while on the opposite side of the square, its attractive modern replacement, the **Casa de sa Constitució**, was built from local sandstone.

Sa Tanca Vell

c/Eivissa, 100m south of Plaça de sa Constitució. Sant Francesc's second chapel, the primitive fourteenth-century Sa Tanca Vell, is worth a quick visit. Barely 5m long by 2m high and topped with a simple barrel-vaulted roof, it was originally constructed in 1362 from rough sandstone blocks, and the partly ruined remains were rebuilt in 1697, when Formentera was resettled. Sa Tanca Vell must have been a horrendously claustrophobic place to take Mass or seek refuge from pirates, with just enough space for a congregation of a dozen or so. After the resettlement, it served as the island's only place of worship for thirty years, until the much larger Església de Sant Francesc

Xavier was completed. Today, the building is fenced in and not open to the public, but you can get a clear enough view of the exterior through the protective railings.

Museu Etnològic

100m northwest of Plaça de sa Constitució on c/Sant Jaume. Mon–Sat 10am–2pm. Free. Sant Francesc's modest Museu Etnològic, situated above a little cultural centre, has a moderately interesting collection of highly polished old farming tools and fishing gear. There are also a few curious old photographs of the island, including one from the early twentieth century of a very muddy, desolate-looking Sant Francesc. Outside the museum is the tiny toy-town steam train that used to shunt the island's salt to the docks from the saltpans.

Cala Saona

South of Sant Francesc, an undulating, ruler-straight main road runs for 2.5km to a signposted branch road that veers west through rust-red fields of carob and fig, and small coppices of aleppo pine, to the appealing bay of Cala Saona, 3km from the junction. The only cove beach in Formentera (and a fairly busy spot in the summer), Cala Saona has temptingly turquoise water, and fine sand that extends 100m back from the coast to the big *Hotel Cala Saona*, the bay's only substantial building.

There are some excellent cliffside walking routes south of here, along coastal paths that meander past sabina pines and sand dunes and offer plenty of quiet, shady spots for a picnic lunch. The sunset views from this section of the coast are stunning, with a dramatic perspective over the Mediterranean to the sphinx-like contours of Es Vedrà and Es Vedranell, and to the soaring hills of southern Ibiza; on exceptionally clear days you can make out the jagged mountains around Dénia on the mainland.

Barbària peninsula ruins

Continuing south from the Cala Saona turn-off, the road

▼ CALA SAONA

▲ CAP DE BARBÀRIA

gradually begins its ascent of Formentera's southern plateau, the sparsely populated Barbària peninsula. Along the route there are a collection of minor archeological sites, all signposted from the road. First are the ruined, fenced-off remnants of the 3800-year-old Bronze Age **Barbària II**, which contained nine simple limestone buildings – bedrooms, workrooms, a kiln and animal quarters. It's beautifully located amidst small arid fields dotted with carob trees and dense patches of pine, which serve as prime habitats for birdlife, including flycatchers and the exotic, zebra-striped hoopoe.

The other sets of remains, **Barbària III** and **Barbària I**, also date from the Bronze Age. Barbària III's singularly unremarkable buildings may have been animal pens while Barbària I consists of a three-metre-wide circular formation of upended stone blocks that may have represented a place of worship, although practically nothing is known about their significance.

Cap de Barbària

The southernmost point in the Pitiuses forms an eerily beautiful, almost lunar landscape. This isolated region, the Cap de Barbària, or "Barbary Cape", is named after the North African pirates who passed this way to plunder the Balearics. The bleak, sun-bleached landscape, dotted with tiny green patches of hardy rosemary and thyme, boasted a dense pine wood until the 1930s, when ruined emigrés, returning to a jobless Formentera during the American Depression, chopped down the trees to make charcoal.

At the end of the road a white-painted lighthouse, the **Far des Barbària**, stands above the swirling, cobalt-blue waters of the Mediterranean, and from here you can spot gulls, shearwaters and perhaps even peregrine falcons. If you pick your way 100m south of the lighthouse, you'll find a cave, **Sa Cova Foradada**, which is worth a quick look. You enter by lowering yourself into a small hole in the roof of the modest single chamber; once you're inside, you can edge your way to the mouth of the cave, almost 100m above the sea, for a stunning view of the Mediterranean. Full-moon parties are sometimes held here in the summer, if the police are not tipped off. The *cova* features in the film *Sex and Lucia*, which was shot in Formentera.

Northeast of the lighthouse, it's a ten-minute walk over to **Torre des Garroveret**, a well-preserved, two-storey eighteenth-century tower. As Formentera's first line of defence against Barbary pirates, it would have been manned night and day in centuries past, but is no longer open. Formenterans claim that on exceptionally clear days it's possible to see the mountains of North Africa from here, despite the fact that they're 110km away.

Sant Ferran

Bus from La Savina, May–Oct 15 daily; Nov–April 3 daily; 10min. Strung out along a busy junction on the main La Savina–La Mola highway, Sant Ferran ("San Fernando" in Castilian), Formentera's second largest town, has an abundance of banks, bars, stores and restaurants. With its two main streets plagued by traffic noise and lined with unsteady-looking apartment blocks, first impressions are not great. But the most attractive part of town, hidden away a couple of streets northeast of the main highway, is well worth

investigating, centred around the pleasantly austere village church, **Església de Sant Ferran**. The church was originally built close to the island's saltpans towards the end of the eighteenth century but poor construction methods and the unsuitability of the sandy terrain meant that the structure started to crumble; in 1883 it was taken down, and over the next six years was reconstructed stone by stone in today's location. Uniquely in the Pitiuses, its simple sandstone facade, topped with a crude belfry, has not been plastered or whitewashed.

Opposite the church is a spacious, paved **plaza**, lined with seats and young palm trees. There's barely a soul to be seen here for most of the year, but during the summer months it becomes a meeting place for young Formenterans and holidaying teenagers. The more mature can be found just down the road at the *Fonda Pepe* (see p.166) or eating at one of the string of restaurants south of the plaza.

Es Pujols

Bus from La Savina, May–Oct 15 daily; Nov–April 3 daily; 15min. Formentera's only designated resort, Es Pujols, 2km north

▼ ES PUJOL

▲ CA NA COSTA

of Sant Ferran, is an attractive, small-scale affair, popular with young Germans and Italians. It's lively but not too boisterous, with a decent quota of bars and a chic little club. Curving off to the northwest, in front of the clump of hotels and apartment blocks, is the reason why virtually everyone is here: the **beach** – two crescents of fine white sand, separated by a low rocky coastal shelf and dotted with ramshackle fishing huts. The beautiful shallow, turquoise water here heats up to tropical temperatures by August, when it can get very crowded, with rows of sunbeds packing the sands. There's nothing much to see away from the beach, and most visitors spend the evening wandering along the promenade, selecting a seafront restaurant and browsing the market stalls.

The summer bar scene is as energetic as you'll get in Formentera, though the odd venue aside, the music is standard-issue Mediterranean holiday mixes. It's not difficult to find the action, mostly centred on c/Espardell just off the promenade and in the streets behind. The hippest spot in town is the *Xueño* club (see p.166).

Ca Na Costa

Bus from Es Pujols, May–Oct 5 daily; 2min. A kilometre northwest of Es Pujols, signposted just off the road to the Salines saltpans and overlooking the waters of Estany Pudent, is the fenced-off megalithic tomb of Ca Na Costa. This tiny but archeologically important site represents the earliest proof of human habitation in Formentera, consisting of a stone circle of upright limestone slabs, up to 2m high, surrounded by concentric circles of smaller stones. These stand adjacent to a mass grave, where the skeletons of eight men and two women have been found – one of the male specimens, at some 2m tall, is thought to have sufferered from gigantism. Archeologists have also unearthed flint tools – not found anywhere else in the Pitiuses – here and ceramic fragments indicating that early Formenterans were trading with Mallorca, suggesting a relatively sophisticated early society with established trade routes.

Salines saltpans

Formentera's shimmering saltpans lie at the very top of the island. They haven't been in commercial use since 1984 (unlike their equivalent on Ibiza – see p.142), but crystallization in the steely-blue pools continues nevertheless, with foam-like clusters of salt clinging to the fringes of the low stone walls that divide the pans. As an extension to Estany Pudent and Estany des Peix, the saltpans form an important wetland zone, attracting gulls, terns, waders and flamingoes, the latter encouraged (or perhaps confused) by the presence of two dozen pink concrete impostors. The pans and surrounding coastal region of northern Formentera, as well as southern Ibiza and Espalmador, are included within a protected "natural park" where building is prohibited.

Platja des Canyers and Platja de sa Roqueta

Bus from La Savina, May–Oct 6 daily; 10min. One kilometre north of Ca Na Costa along the road that skirts the east coast, a signposted turn-off on the right leads to two neighbouring sandy bays, Platja des Canyers and Platja de sa Roqueta. They're not amongst Formentera's most scenic beaches, but both offer good swimming in calm, shallow water and have kiosks selling refreshments.

Es Cavall and the Molí des Carregador

Just west of the saltpans, the slender, sandy beach of Es Cavall (sometimes called Cala Savina) has two excellent but pricey *chiringuitos* – *Big Sur* and *Tiburón* – and great swimming, as well as some shade from the coastal pines. Just north of the beach, along a sandy track, there's a huge old windmill, Molí des Carregador, which used to pump sea water into the saltpans – it's now been converted into a mediocre but expensive seafood restaurant.

Trucador peninsula

A slender finger of low-lying land, the idyllic Trucador peninsula extends north towards the island of Espalmador.

Virtually the entire length of this sandy promontory, part of Ses Salines Natural Park, is blessed with exquisite beaches lapped by shallow waters. From the Molí des Carregador windmill, a sandy track heads north through steep sand dunes, passing a turn-off on the right for a short path that twists around the tip of the saltpans eastwards to **Platja Llevant**, a glorious undeveloped beach that forms the east coast of the Trucador peninsula – this eye-dazzling stretch of white sand is also where you'll find the large, popular *Tango* beach restaurant.

Continuing northwards up the peninsula, the sandy track eventually ends beside a huge car park packed with hundreds of scooters and bicycles in high season. Just offshore are two small islets, **Pouet** and **Rodona**, that give this slim stretch of beach its name: **Platja Illetes**. The sands here are very popular with day-trippers from Ibiza in high season, when you can rent windsurfing equipment from a beachside hut.

You'll have to continue on foot if you want to explore the very narrow final section of the peninsula, which is barely 30m wide and bordered by blinding white powdery sand that never seems to get too busy.

These back-to-back beaches are Formentera's very best, with astonishingly clear, turquoise-tinged water on both sides of the slim, sandy finger of land. A kilometre from the car park, you reach the northerly tip of Formentera, **Es Pas**, or "The Crossing", partially connected to the island of Espalmador by a 300-metre sand bar. If the sea is not too choppy, you should be able to cross over without soaking your belongings.

Espalmador

A shelf-like island of dunes and sandstone rock, most people visit Espalmador for stunning **s'Alga beach**, with its sublime, shallow water and fine arc of white sand. In summer, the sheltered bay bristles with yachts, and is a favoured destination for day-trippers from Ibiza (many of the Formentera-bound boat-trips from Ibiza stop here on their way to La Savina). Some visitors take time out to visit the **sulphurous mud pond** a few minutes' walk north of the beach – you'll probably have it to yourself if you visit early or late in the day. The entire crust of the four-hectare pool has dried out considerably in recent years because of declining rainfall, but, even in the height of summer, there are three or four small patches of softer mud that you can climb down to for a good writhe around in gooey bliss. The one monument, the aptly named **Torre de sa Guardiola** ("Piggy-bank Tower"), on the western flank of the island, is a two-storey eighteenth-century defence tower – with a slot-like opening on its flank – clearly visible from the decks of ferries heading to Ibiza.

Cova d'en Xeroni

May–Oct 10am–2pm & 5–8pm. €4. Southeast of Sant Ferran, Formentera's main highway descends towards a central isthmus only a couple of kilometres wide in places. Just off the highway at the 6km marker, there's a signposted turn-off for Cova d'en Xeroni, a large limestone cave consisting of a single, forty-metre-wide cavern that was accidentally discovered in the 1970s when the owner of the land started drilling for a well. His son now conducts regular tours

▼ MUD POND, ESPALMADOR

of the chamber's spiky crop of stalactites and stalagmites, though only in German, Italian, Spanish or Catalan. The tour has a certain kitsch appeal, as the owners have lit the cavern with 1970s disco lights, but unless you're interested in gawping at vaguely Santa Claus-like formations, it's not really worth the bother.

Platja de Migjorn

Vying with the Trucador beaches for status as Formentera's finest strip of sand, Platja de Migjorn ("Midday Beach") is a wonderful six-kilometre swathe of pale sand washed by gleaming, azure water, extending along the entire south coast of Formentera's central strip. Most of it is more or less pristine, with development confined to the extremities – at the western end, **Es Ca Marí**, signposted 3km south of Sant Ferran, is a loose scattering of hotel blocks set back from the sand, while at the eastern end, Mar i Land comprises two large hotels (see opposite). To get to the best stretch of sand, turn south off the highway at the 8km marker, where a bumpy dirt track passes through picturesque fields of wheat and fig trees separated by Formentera's characteristic dry-stone walls. You'll emerge at the sea beside the sand dunes that spread back from the shore, adjacent to *Lucky* (see p.164) and the legendary *Blue Bar* (see p.165).

Castell Romà de Can Blai

Around the 10km marker on the highway through Formentera's central strip, a signposted turn-off leads just south to the fenced-in remains of a large Roman fort, Castell Romà de Can Blai. The sandstone foundations are all that's left of the square structure, which originally had five towers. The fort guarded the island's east–west highway and the nearby port, Es Caló de Sant Agustí, but little else is known about it.

Es Caló de Sant Agustí

Bus from La Savina, May–Oct 7 daily; Nov–April 1 daily, 15min. Nestled around a rocky niche in the north coast, 2km east of the Castell Romà, the tiny cove of Es Caló de Sant Agustí has served as nearby La Mola's fishing port since Roman times.

▼ PLATJA DE MIGJORN

Sitting snug below the cliffs of La Mola, this diminutive harbour consists of a tiny, rocky, semicircular bay ringed by the rails of fishing huts. It's a pretty enough scene, but there's no real reason to stop other than for Es Caló's two excellent fish restaurants, *Rafalet* (see p.165) and *Pascual* (see p.165).

The shallow water surrounding Es Caló does offer decent snorkelling; head for the heavily eroded limestone rocks that ring the bay to the south. If you're after a beach, scramble 300m over the rocks (or take the signposted turn-off from the highway) to the inviting sands at **Ses Platgetes**, where you'll also find a good *kiosko* selling snacks and drinks.

La Mola

See p.150 for details of buses. The knuckle-shaped tableland of La Mola, the island's eastern tip, is the most scenic part of Formentera, combining dense forest with traditionally farmed countryside. La Mola's limestone promontory looks down on the rest of the island from a high point of 192m, and there are stunning views across the ocean from the steep cliffs that have given the area's inhabitants protection on three sides since it was first settled around 2000 BC.

From Es Caló de Sant Agustí, the highway dips before beginning the long climb, passing a signposted left turn after 500m for Camí Romà, a beautiful but steep pathway up to La Mola which was part of the original Roman road across Formentera. It offers hikers a refreshingly shady and traffic-free shortcut up the hill. The highway's steep incline continues past the Mar i Land turn-off, winding through Formentera's largest forest via a

▲ ESGLÉSIA DEL PILAR DE LA MOLA

series of hairpin bends that will exhaust all but the fittest cyclists. At the 14km marker is the *El Mirador* restaurant (see p.165), from where there are sublime sunset views, after which the road levels out.

Mar i Land

Bus from La Savina, May–Oct 7 daily; Nov–April 1 daily; 20min. Close to the highway's 13km marker, you can turn off right for the upmarket enclave of Mar i Land (also spelled "Maryland"), where two huge hotel complexes spill down a hillside towards the easternmost section of Platja de Migjorn beach (see opposite). This section of shoreline, known as **Es Arenals**, is usually the most crowded spot on the southern coast. Although there are lifeguards on duty here between May and September, take care if you go for a swim, as the currents can be unpredictable.

El Pilar de la Mola

Bus from La Savina via Sant Francesc, May–Oct 4 daily; Nov–April 1 daily; extra service on market days at 5pm from La Savina via Sant Francesc, Sant Ferran and Es Pujols, return service leaves La Mola at 7pm; 25min. The region's solitary village, and a social centre for the farmers and bohemian types who make up most of the area's population, El Pilar de la Mola is a modest, pleasantly unspoiled settlement of around fifty houses, a handful of stores and a few simple bar-cafés strung along the main highway. Most of the time it's a subdued little place, though there's a flurry of activity on Wednesdays and Sundays in the summer season, when an **art market** (May to late Sept 4–9pm) is held in the village's small central plaza. Much of the jewellery and craftwork is made locally, and tends to be far more imaginative than a lot of the junk on sale in Ibizan hippy markets; there's usually some live music towards the end of the day as well.

Two hundred metres east of the market plaza is the village church, **Església del Pilar de la Mola**. Built between 1772 and 1784 to a typically Ibizan design, it's the usual minimalist, whitewashed Pitiusan edifice, with a single-arched side porch and a simple belfry.

The only other sights around La Mola are two ancient **windmills** on the eastern outskirts, formerly used for grinding wheat. By the 1960s, these windmills had fallen into disuse and became hippy communes – Bob Dylan is said to have lived inside eighteenth-century **Molí Vell** for several months. Though you can't go inside the windmill today, it has been well restored and its warped wooden sails are still capable of turning the grindstone.

Far de la Mola

It's a quick straight dash through flat farmland, planted with hardy vines, to the Far de la Mola lighthouse, set in glorious

▲ FAR DE LA MOLA

seclusion at Formentera's easternmost point, Punta de la Mola. The whitewashed structure, which has a 37-kilometre beam, is something of a local landmark, and was the inspiration for the "lighthouse at the end of the world" in Jules Verne's novel *Journey Around the Solar System*. Verne was obviously taken by the wild isolation of the site, and there's a stone monument to him beside the house. There's also an excellent café-bar here, *Es Puig* (see p.166).

Hotels

Las Banderas

Platja de Migjorn ☎604 644 832, ℮lasbanderas@terra.es. April–Oct. Right on Platja de Migjorn beach, this hotel-restaurant hangout has a choice of bungalow-style digs or rooms, all simply furnished with shabby-chic artistic touches. It's pricey for what you get, but the location and ambience makes *Las Banderas* popular, so book ahead. The nearest bus stop is about 1km away so you may want to rent a bike or a scooter. €85.

Cap de Barbària

Cap de Barbària ☎617 460 629, ⓦwww.capdebarbaria.com.
Formentera's first *agroturismo*, this spectacular ultra-luxurious rustic hideaway has every mod con that you could dream up. The six huge rooms have beamed ceilings, air con and fireplaces, and there's a top-drawer restaurant, open to non-residents (daily 8–10.30pm), with a French Med menu, 16-metre pool and sea views. Only for the seriously minted. €460.

Hostal La Savina

Avgda Mediterránea 22–40, La Savina ☎971 322 279, ⓔhostallasavina@terra .es. May–Oct. This large hotel does not look that appealing from the exterior (and it's on the main road out of town) but it's actually a well-managed place with very helpful staff and good facilities, including access to a narrow beach area that faces the Estany des Peix. Rooms are bright and comfortable, all with air con and attractive bathrooms, and many have lake views (for an extra charge). A buffet breakfast is included (served in the ground floor bar/restaurant) and there's also Internet access. €77–92.

▼ LAS BANDERAS

Hostal Residencia Illes Pitiüses

Ctra La Savina–La Mola, Sant Ferran ☎971 328 189, ⓦwww.illespitiuses .com. It's no longer a bargain, but this modern hotel has 26 recently renovated and spacious rooms, all with satellite TV, air con, safe and private bathroom. The location, on the main cross-island road, is not great, though traffic noise isn't that noticeable. The café downstairs serves good grub and has a sunny rear terrace. €75–103.

Hostal Residencia Mar Blau

Es Caló de Sant Agustí ☎971 327 030. April–Oct. A cheery little place in a remote spot next to a tiny fishing harbour and near Ses Platgetes beach. The attractive rooms are good value and there are also similar-quality apartments next door that sleep up to four (the latter costing from €98). €74–92.

Hostal Residencia Mayans

Es Pujols ☎971 328 724. May–Oct. Pleasant *hostal* in a quiet spot 100m away from the main resort area. The rooms are bright, modern and agreeably decorated and all have private bathrooms; book one on the upper floors for panoramic sea or island views. There's a pool, and the terrace café downstairs serves a popular buffet breakfast. €74.

Pensions

Pension Bon Sol

c/Major 84–90, Sant Ferran ☎971 328 882. April–Oct. One of the cheapest places on Formentera, this simple *pension* is just south of Sant Ferran's plaza. Offers clean, basic, fairly large rooms above a friendly bar; bathrooms are shared. €34.

PLACES Formentera

Shops

Formentera Tattoo

c/d'Espardell, Es Pujols. Stocks surf and club wear and jewellery, and has an in-store tattoo parlour.

Summertime

c/Pla de Rei 59, Sant Francesc Xavier. Fashion boutique with a selection of colourful, stylish summer gear for women.

Cafés

Café Martinal

c/Archiduc Salvador 18, Sant Francesc Xavier. Mon–Sat 8am–3pm. Your best bet for breakfast in Sant Francesc, this enjoyable place has a choice of set menus that include fresh juices, cereals and mini-*bocadillos*.

Cafeteria Espardell

Passeig Marítim, Es Pujols. Daily 8.30am–11pm. A traditional café and *pastelería*, with filling set breakfasts, modestly priced meals and a huge selection of cakes, pastries and tarts. It faces the beach on Es Pujol's promenade.

Fonda Platé

c/Santa Maria, Sant Francesc Xavier. Mon–Sat 10am–1am. Inviting place with a great vine-shaded terrace facing Sant Francesc's pretty central square. There's also a lofty, beamed interior with pinball, pool and bar football. The extensive menu includes tapas, salads, pasta and good juices.

Lucky

Platja de Migjorn. May–Oct daily 10am–sunset. Inexpensive and consistently good Italian-run beach place that's ideal for a light lunch with a view. Offers well-prepared salads, fresh fish and pasta plus languid background chillout sounds. To get here, take the turn-off at km 8 on the La Savina–La Mola road.

Restaurants

Flipper & Chiller

Platja de Migjorn ☎971 187 596, ⓦwww.flipperandchiller.com. May–Oct daily noon–1am. Occupying pole position at the eastern end of Platja de Migjorn, this zany new place has an ocean-facing deck and a lounge zone scattered

▼ CAFÉ MARTINAL

with pink sofas. The menu is modern, with creatively-assembled salads (try the king crab), rice dishes and meat and fish choices. With a wine list running at fifty-plus bottles, and twelve cavas, you won't go thirsty, even if your wallet runs dry (a mixed fruit juice is €7).

El Mirador

La Savina–La Mola road, km 14 ☎971 327 037. May–Oct daily 1–4pm & 7–11pm. This popular, moderately priced spot has jaw-dropping views over the entire western half of the island from its terrace, and an inexpensive menu – the *ensalada de bescuit* (prepared with local bread and dried fish) is a Formenteran speciality and the paellas and grilled meats are also excellent.

La Pequeña Isla

El Pilar de la Mola ☎971 327 068. May–Oct 1–4pm & 8–11.30pm; Nov–April 7.30–11pm. Reliable village bar-restaurant, known for its well-prepared local dishes – roast rabbit, sausages, squid – as well as couscous and rice-based meals. Eat on the covered outside terrace, or in the dining area at the rear.

Restaurant Pascual

Caló de Sant Agustí ☎971 327 014. April–Oct 1–4pm & 7–11pm. Consistently recommended by locals, this seafood restaurant has been run by the same team for years. There's no sea view, but for around €25–30 per person you can feast on terrific spiny (or Norwegian) lobster or the paella-like *arròs a la banda* on a terrace underneath pine trees.

Restaurant Rafalet

Caló de Sant Agustí ☎971 327 077. May–Sept daily 1–4pm & 7–11.30pm. Right next to *Restaurant Pascual*,

▲ FLIPPER & CHILLER

this excellent place offers two separate dining options. The casual, inexpensive bar area's speciality is *pa amb coses* ("bread and things") which may include ham, tortilla, olives and cheese and other tapas, for around €12 per person. *Rafalet*'s other half is an elegant, fairly formal fish restaurant where the tables have views of the sea and Es Caló bay. The menu includes grilled *bollit de peix* (a rice dish with red mullet) and local fish like mero and dorado.

Bars

Bar Verdera

Sant Ferran. Daily 6.30am–1.30am. Also known as *Los Currantes*, this unreconstructed, scruffy locals' bar initially looks pretty unappealing but it does have an excellent and very inexpensive selection of tapas. It's right on the main highway with roadside seating.

Blue Bar

Platja de Migjorn ☎971 187 011, ⊛www.bluebarformentera.com. April–Oct daily noon–4am. Once the definitive hippy beach hangout in Formentera, today

▲ BLUE BAR

the *Blue Bar* is something of an ambient HQ, where DJs beam out seamless electronic music across the decked terrace – quite an experience under Formentera's star-filled night skies. The restaurant here (open until midnight) serves up fresh fish and pasta, though be prepared to wait for your food. Get here via the signposted turn-off at km 7.9 on the La Savina–La Mola road.

Fonda Pepe
c/Major, Sant Ferran. May–Oct & Christmas–New Year daily 8am–3am. Another bar that's steeped in hippy folklore, this idiosyncratic drinking den still flies the flag for flower power, its walls covered with photos and doodles from the 1960s. In summer its narrow terrace is packed with (mainly German) visitors revelling in the trippy nostalgia. The adjoining *Peyka* restaurant is open for dinner only.

Es Puig
Punta de la Mola. Daily May–Oct 9am–10pm; Nov–April 9am–6pm. The bar at the end of the world, right next to the Far de la Mola lighthouse, and famous for its *platos de jamón y queso* – huge portions of local and Menorcan cheese, cured ham and salami. It's also *the* place to wait for the first sunrise of the New Year, when the bar stays open all night.

Clubs

Xueño
Es Pujols–Sant Ferran road ⓦ www .xueno.com. June–Sept. Stylish, well-regarded club, owned and run by Italians with excellent connections to the global house scene. DJs David Morales and Bob Sinclar, and singers Barbara Tucker and Robert Owens have all performed here, alongside regular DJs Buti and Claudio Coccoluto. It's an intimate place (the capacity is around 400), with stylish decor, a powerful sound system in the main room and a terrace and chillout zone. Draws a mixed Italian/local crowd; entrance and bar prices are fairly moderate.

▼ XUEÑO

Essentials

Arrival

Ibiza Airport (☎ 971 809 000) is 7km south of Ibiza Town. Buses run to Ibiza Town all year round (#10; hourly 7.30am–10.30pm; €1.30), and there are also summer services to Sant Antoni (#9; June–Sept 7 daily, 30 min; €1.75) and Santa Eulària (#24; May–Oct 7 daily, 30min; €0.75). You can check the latest schedules on ☎ www.ibizabus.com.

Taxis charge approximately €13 to Ibiza Town, €22 to Sant Antoni or €25 to Santa Eulària; prices rise a little after 9pm. Virtually all package holidays include a free transfer to your hotel. There's no airport in **Formentera**, but regular ferries and hydrofoils shuttle

between the two islands, mostly from Ibiza Town (see p.51).

International **ferries** from mainland Spain (Barcelona, Dénia, Valencia and Alicante) dock at Passeig Marítim on the south side of Ibiza Town's harbour, and at the harbourfront dock in Sant Antoni. At the time of writing there was also a direct weekly ferry to La Savina, Formentera.

Note that travel connections to both islands are much poorer in **winter**. At the time of research there were no direct flights to Ibiza from the UK between November and April, when it's best to travel via Palma, Barcelona or Madrid.

Information and maps

The best information about Ibiza and Formentera is available from tourist information offices on the islands, and via the Internet. There are **tourist offices** at the airport (May–Sept Mon–Sat 9am–2pm & 4–9pm, Sun 9am–2pm; ☎ 971 809 118), in Ibiza Town (see p.51), in Sant Antoni (see p.109) and Santa Eulària (see p.80), in addition to the small kiosks (all May–Oct only) located in many resorts. There's also a helpful office in La Savina, Formentera (see p.152). All staff speak English, and can provide leaflets and accommodation lists.

On the **Web**, try the excellent Ibiza Spotlight (☎ www.ibiza-spotlight.com) or ☎ www.guiaformentera.com for Formentera. Ibiza Voice (☎ www.ibiza-voice.com) has good features, listings and content about the club scene. The Balearic Islands' website (☎ www.visitbalears.com) is worth a look, with features, news and events in separate sections devoted to Ibiza and Formentera.

The Spanish Tourist Board (☎ www.tourspain.es) only has very general background detail about the Pitiuses.

All the main British **newspapers** are widely available, and a few international titles. For local news, the DIY journalism peddled by the *Ibiza Sun* (☎ www.theibizasun.com), a free newspaper available in all resorts, covers the main stories in reasonable depth (though the editorial tone can be rabid at times); the somewhat pedestrian monthly *Ibiza Now* is geared towards the ageing expat market. Check out the excellent glossy magazine *Pacha* for features on Ibizan life, club culture and island personalities.

The best **map** of Ibiza is published by Kompass (1:50,000). Of those available in Ibiza, Joan Costa (1:70,000) is the one to go for. Most car rental companies will provide you with a reasonable free map. Serious hikers should pick up copies of the IGN 1:25,000 maps, available at Transit, c/d'Aragó 45, Ibiza Town.

Transport

Ibiza has a pretty good transport network, with regular public **buses** and **boats** linking all the main resorts and towns, and there's a decent bus service on Formentera considering its tiny population. If you're planning on really exploring the islands, however, you're going to have to rent a **car**, **motorbike** or a **bicycle**, as many of the best stretches of coastline are well off the beaten track.

Buses

Buses in Ibiza and Formentera are inexpensive, punctual, and will get you around fairly quickly. Services between the main towns and resorts run roughly from 7.30am to midnight between June and late September, and 7.30am until 9.30pm in winter. Smaller villages and resorts are less well served, and buses to them are very infrequent in winter. Conversely, services to the more popular beaches and resorts are increased between June and late September. **Timetables** are available in tourist offices, printed in local newspapers and available at ⓦ www .ibizabus.com. Note that there are many fewer buses on Sundays on all routes.

From **Ibiza Town**, there are buses to all the main towns, most villages and many resorts, and to Salines Beach, all year round. **Sant Antoni** and **Santa Eulària** are the other two transport hubs, with frequent services to local beach resorts and good intra-island connections. In **Formentera**, buses shuttle between Es Pujols, Sant Ferran, Sant Francesc and La Savina, and there's also a route across the island, from La Savina to La Mola. **Fares** are very reasonable on all routes: Ibiza Town–Sant Antoni costs €1.80, while the longest route, Ibiza Town–Portinatx, is €3.

Between mid-June and late September the all-night **discobus** service provides hourly shuttles between Ibiza Town and Sant Antoni (stopping at *Amnesia* and *Privilege*); Ibiza Town and Platja d'en Bossa (for *Space*); Sant Antoni and Port des Torrent; Es Canar and Santa Eulària; and Santa Eulària and Ibiza Town. During the rest of the year, the same buses run on Saturday nights only. Tickets cost €2.20; for more information, call ☏ 971 192 456.

Tourist train

Kids will love the "tourist train", a mock steam locomotive with carriages that runs on four different routes around Ibiza. From Es Canar beach, there's a choice of three routes: two include the village of Sant Carles and east-coast cove beaches, and another runs to Santa Eulària. Possibly the most interesting excursion leaves from Portinatx, taking in Cala de Sant Vicent and the cave of Cova Marçà at Port de Sant Miquel. Prices start at €8 for adults and €5 for under-12s. For more information, consult ⓦ www.trenturisticoibiza.com or call ☏ 607 654 321.

Boats

Plenty of **boats** buzz up and down the Ibizan coastline between May and late September, providing a delightful – if expensive – alternative to bus travel. Services go from Ibiza Town to Talamanca and Platja d'en Bossa; from Sant Antoni to Sant Antoni Bay, Cala Bassa and Cala Conta; and from Santa Eulària to the beaches of the northeast, including Es Canar. Fares range from €3–7. For ferry and hydrofoil connections between Ibiza Town and Formentera, see p.152.

Taxis

Taxi rates on both islands are quite pricey, though all have meters and tariffs are fixed. There's a minimum charge of €3.90, with additional charges after 9pm, on Sundays and public holidays, and to or from the airport or docks. Ibiza Town to Sant Antoni (15km) will cost about €19, while to get to Sant Rafel (for *Amnesia* or *Privilege*) from either Ibiza Town or Sant Antoni at night is around €13. The latest fares are posted on ⓦwww.taxi-eivissa.com.

Taxis for hire display a green light – you can hail them on the street, wait at one of the designated ranks, or call (see numbers on below). You'll have few problems getting a taxi at most times of the year, but demand far exceeds supply on most August nights, when it's possible to have to wait for up to an hour for a ride – avoid the cowboy taxi-drivers who hustle for business in high season; most are uninsured.

From the airport, there are often huge queues at busy arrival times, though the line does go down pretty quickly. It's well worth bearing in mind that all Ibizan clubs will pay your taxi fare from anywhere on the island if four of the passengers buy an entrance ticket to the venue.

Taxi companies
Ibiza Town ⓣ971 398 483, ⓣ971 301 794, ⓣ971 306 602.
La Savina, Formentera ⓣ971 322 002.
Sant Antoni ⓣ971 340 074, ⓣ971 343 764.
Santa Eulària ⓣ971 330 063.
Sant Francesc, Formentera ⓣ971 322 016.
Sant Joan ⓣ971 800 243.
Es Pujols, Formentera ⓣ971 328 016.

Car and motorbike rental

Driving along Ibiza's and Formentera's main roads is pretty straightforward, though to really see the islands you'll have to tackle some challenging dirt tracks from time to time. Take particular care on unlit highways, including the roads to Sant Josep and Sant Joan, at night, where fatal accidents are all too common.

Daily **car-rental** costs are reasonable: for the cheapest small hatchback, expect to pay around €38 a day in July and August, and around €30 per day over the rest of the year. Local companies are usually less expensive than the international brands. Note that it's essential to book a car in advance in August due to high demand. You have to be over 21 to rent a car in Spain.

Motorbikes and **scooters** are also a popular means of getting around the islands independently, with rates starting at around €30 for the cheapest motorbike, or from €22 a day for a scooter model. In low-lying Formentera, even the least powerful model will be adequate to get two people around, but to explore hilly Ibiza you should rent a machine above 100cc. Legally, you must be over 18 to rent a motorbike over 75cc, and crash helmets are compulsory.

Vehicle **insurance policies** vary but it's essential to ensure you have full cover (all the companies listed on below include this in their contracts). Check the excess waiver amount – obviously, the higher the rate specified in the contract, the more you'll have to pay if you're involved in an accident. Note that most insurance policies cover you for neither breakdowns nor accidents on dirt roads.

Guardia Civil patrols frequently use breathalizers to test drivers' alcohol consumption. It's not uncommon for patrols to stop every other vehicle leaving the big clubs' car parks in summer. The legal limit in Spain is 0.5 milligrams of alcohol per millilitre of blood, stricter than the UK's maximum of 0.8 milligrams.

Local car and motorbike rental companies
Class Avgda Cala Llonga, Cala Llonga ⓣ971 196 285 & Avgda Cala Nova, Es Canar ⓣ971 338 028; ⓦwww.class-rentacar.com.
Moto Luis Avgda Portmany 5, Sant Antoni ⓣ971 340 521, ⓦwww.motoluis.com.
Isla Blanca c/Felipe II, Ibiza Town ⓣ971 315 407; La Savina, Formentera ⓣ971 322 559.

International car rental companies
All the offices below are located at Ibiza Airport.
Avis ⓣ971 396 453, ⓦwww.avis.com.
Budget ⓣ971 395 982, ⓦwww.budget.com.
Hertz ⓣ971 396 018, ⓦwww.hertz.com.
National ⓣ971 395 393, ⓦwww.nationalcar.com.

Cycling

With few hills, **Formentera** is perfect bicycle territory and **cycling** is an easy and popular way to get around the island. Pick up a *Green Routes* leaflet from the tourist office for details of some good, well-signposted cycle excursions along the island's quieter lanes. **Ibiza** is much hillier, and its roads more congested, though there are some spectacular dirt-track routes across the island, perfect for mountain biking. A network of signposted routes is currently being developed; contact tourist information offices for leaflets. In both islands, renting bikes starts at around €8 a day, while state-of-the-art mountain bikes cost from €10 and kids' bikes around €7.

Kandani (see below) and Ecoibiza, c/Abad i Lasierra 35, Ibiza Town (☎ 971 302 347, ⓦ www.ecoibiza .com), organize **mountain-bike tours**. Ecoibiza's half-day excursions start at €37 and a tour of Formentera costs €52. ⓦ www.ibizabtt.com has details of serious mountain-biking events.

Bike rental

Autos Ca Marí La Savina, Formentera ☎971 322 921.

Bicicletas/Moto Rent Mitjorn La Savina, Formentera ☎971 322 306.

Kandani Ctra Es Canar 109, Santa Eulària ☎ & ⓕ971 339 264, ⓦwww.kandani.com.

Tony Rent c/Navarra 11, Ibiza Town ☎971 300 879.

Sports and leisure

You'll find plenty of opportunity for **sports and leisure activities** in Ibiza and Formentera, from yoga to horse riding. With a sparkling coastline never more than a short drive away, watersports are especially popular. Coastal Ibiza and Formentera also offer superb scenery for hikers.

Swimming and beach life

Swimming in Ibiza and Formentera is absolutely wonderful, with dozens of Blue Flag beaches and unpolluted, clear and – for much of the year – warm water to enjoy. Sea temperatures are at their lowest in February (around 15°C), and highest in early September (around 25°C).

All resort beaches, and most family-oriented bays have umbrellas (€3–5 per day) and sunbeds (€3–5 per day) for rent, though at Salines you can get stung for as much as €8 a bed. You'll also find pedalos (around €8 per hour), and many beaches, including Cala Bassa (see p.119)

and Platja d'en Bossa (see p.139), offer banana-boat rides (around €9 per trip).

Diving and snorkelling

The Pitiusan islands boast some of the cleanest seas in the Mediterranean. With little rainfall runoff, the water is exceptionally clear for most of the year and visibility of up to 40m is quite common.

Scuba diving is generally excellent, with warm seas and (mostly) gentle currents. Boats tend to head for the tiny offshore islands, such as Tagomago and Espardell, that ring the coasts, where sea life is at its most diverse. Schools of barracuda and large grouper are often seen, and you can expect to spot conger and moray eels, plenty of colourful wrasse, plus crab and octopus. There are also three shipwrecks around Illot Lladó near Ibiza Town and another in Cala Mastella, plus caves and crevices all around the coastline to investigate. Most scuba-diving schools open between

May and September only (those that open longer are noted below) and tend to charge similar prices. A single boat-dive works out at between €30–45, depending how much equipment you have, and there are discounts for packages of six or ten (or even 100 dives, if you are a group). If you want to **learn to dive**, expect to pay €360–440 for a five-day PADI Open Water course. You'll find a BSAC school in Port des Torrent, and there's a decompression chamber in Ibiza Town.

Small coves and rocky shorelines offer the most productive **snorkelling** territory: try Cala Mastella, Cala Molí and Cala Codolar in Ibiza, or Caló de Sant Agustí in Formentera. Perhaps the best area for experienced snorkellers and freedivers is the rugged northwest Ibizan coastline, at bays such as Es Portitxol and Cala d'Aubarca, where there are very steep drop-offs and deep, clear water. You'll often encounter coastal fish such as ballan, goby, grouper, brown and painted wrasse, as well as passing pelagic sea life such as mackerel or even barracuda. Most resorts have a store where you can buy snorkelling equipment, but as much of it is poor quality, it's well worth renting or buying from a dive school or a specialist fishing store.

Scuba-diving centres

Diving Centre San Miguel *Hotel Cartago*, Port de Sant Miquel ☎971 334 539, ⓦwww.divingcenter-sanmiguel.com. Professional, Formentera-based school that also offers dives on Ibiza sites like Es Vedrà.
Blue Adventure c/Almadrava 67, La Savina, Formentera ☎971 323 297, ⓦwww.blue-adventure.com. Scuba school with inexpensive rates, though not PADI affiliated.
Ibiza Diving Port Esportiu, Santa Eulària ☎971 332 949, ⓦwww.ibiza-diving.com. Five-star PADI school, with Nitrox training courses, and a 12.5m dive boat.
Sea Horse Sub Port des Torrent ☎971 346 438, ⓦwww.seahorsedivingibiza.com. BSAC-accredited school offering dives inside the Cala d'Hort Natural Park. May–Oct.
Subfari Es Portitxol beach, Cala Portinatx ☎971 333 183, ⓦwww.dive-ibiza.com. Scuba school that runs dives at many of Ibiza's remote north-coast sites.

Vellmari Marina Botafoc 101–2, Ibiza Town ☎971 192 884; Avgda Mediterráneo 90, La Savina, Formentera ☎971 322 105; ⓦwww.vellmari.com. Five-star PADI dive centres that offer Nitrox diving and daily trips into the Ses Salines Natural Park; the Ibiza branch is open all year.

Windsurfing, sailing and kayaking

Windsurfing and **sailing** are popular in the Pitiuses – July and August are often the calmest months, so less challenging for the experienced, but conditions are excellent for much of the summer. In early and late summer, the southern sirocco wind reaches Force 4 about once a week, while the westerly mistral can blow in at Force 6. The most popular beaches for windsurfing include Cala Martina (ideal for beginners) just north of Santa Eulària, Platja d'en Bossa and Cala Conta (for the more advanced). Windsurf board rental costs around €18 per hour and training courses around €25 per hour.

Exploring Ibiza's corrugated coastline by **kayak** is an excellent way to get to hidden beaches and remote rocky bays; training courses and excursions can be organized locally.

Windsurfing, sailing and kayak centres

Club de Surf Ibiza Platja d'en Bossa ☎971 192 418. Long-established windsurfing school, offering board rental and tuition.
Club Delfin Vela y Windsurf *Hotel Delfin*, Cala Codolar ☎971 806 210. This sailing school also offers windsurf tuition and board rental.
Ibikayak ☎971 804 050, ⓦwww.ibikayak.com. These kayak specialists run trips to destinations including Es Vedrà and Cala Jondal.
Vela Náutica Avgda Dr Fleming, Sant Antoni ☎971 346 535. Windsurfing equipment, sailing boats and kayaks for rent.

Boat trips and deep-sea fishing

Pleasure-boat trips around the coastline are highly popular, and available in most Ibizan resorts and in the town of Santa

Eulària. The Ibiza to Formentera day-trip is the most popular, costing €20–28 and usually leaving around 9.30am and returning by 6.30pm. Most stop at Espalmador island before continuing to Platja Illetes, and often La Savina. From Ibiza Town, ferries leave from the Formentera terminal, at the north end of the Marina (see map, p.56), while from smaller resorts there are usually deals marked up at the harbour.

Other excursions leaving from Sant Antoni harbour (all bookable from the harbourfront) include a three-hour return trip to Es Vedrà (daily; €16), passing Atlantis and including a snorkelling stop in Cala d'Hort, and a day-trip up the northwest coastline to Portinatx, taking in many isolated coves (twice-weekly; €20 return). In Formentera, Cruceros, La Savina (℡ 971 323 207) organizes excellent half-day (€55 per person) and full-day (€80) trips on a catamaran around the island; prices include a gourmet lunch.

It need not be that expensive to **charter** a boat. The English-owned *The Life of Riley* catamaran (℡ 629 007 356, ⓦ www .sail-ibiza.com; from €95 per head) offers an excellent range of flexible excursions including day-trips to Espalmador and Formentera, with pick-ups from Salines and other Ibiza beaches.

Tagomago Charters, Port Esportiu, Santa Eulària (℡ 971 338 101), have a good choice of vessels from simple tub-like craft with an outboard motor (€220 per day) to swanky Sunseekers (€4000 a day); add on €150 a day for a skipper. Ibiza Med Yachting (℡ 617 078 877, ⓦ www.ibizamed.com) has a great selection of speed boats for hire starting at €1450 per day.

Deep-sea fishing is another popular sport; Pesca Ibiza, Edificio Bristol, Avgda 8 d'Agost, Ibiza Town (℡ 971 314 491), organizes trawling and bottom-fishing excursions from €115 per person for a half-day trip.

Hiking

Ibiza-and Formentera's beautiful coastal paths and inland valleys offer exceptional **hiking**. We've detailed a few of the best walks within the Guide (see pp.102, 131 & 140), all of which have opportunities for a swim along the way; trainers and shorts are adequate equipment. If you plan on doing a lot of walking, IGN (see p.169) publish the most useful maps, and the locally published *Ibiza Now* hiking guides are pretty decent, though only available in Ibiza (from most bookshops and newsagents).

The quality of the Ibizan tourist offices' hiking leaflets is improving but is still not very reliable, though the signpost network that accompanies the routes is helpful. Things are better organized in Formentera, where the Green Routes network has good waymarked tracks suitable for hikers and bikers (leaflets available from the tourist office in La Savina).

Ecoibiza, c/Abad y Lasierra 35, Ibiza Town (℡ 971 302 347, ⓦ www.ecoibiza .com), arranges some good "Secret Walks" to remote parts of the island, including some superb hikes around Santa Agnès to the Torres de Lluc; half-day trips cost from €28 per person; full-day excursions are €34–45.

Horse riding

In Ibiza, Easy Riders (℡ 610 443 630), located 200m along the Sòl d'en Serra from Cala Llonga, has some fine horses and offers thrilling countryside and beach and hill rides; a fifty-minute trek will set you back around €22 while an hour and forty minutes is €40. You could also try Can Mayans, Santa Gertrudis–Sant Llorenç road, km 3 (℡ 971 187 388), who charge from €18 per hour for countryside rides.

Go-karting

There are two **go-kart tracks** in Ibiza; the hilly 300m Santa Eulària circuit, Ibiza Town–Santa Eulària road, km 5.8 (daily March–Oct 10am–sunset; ℡ 971 317 744, ⓦ www.gokartssantaeulalia .com), is the better option, with speedy 400cc adult karts (€22 for 7min), junior karts (€8 for 7min) and baby karts (€4 for 5min). Much flatter and less scenic, Karting San Antonio (daily May–Oct 10am–midnight; ☎ 971 343 805) is just outside Sant Antoni along the highway to Ibiza Town and has similar prices.

Golf

The only **golf** course in the Pitiuses is Club de Golf Ibiza (☎ 971 196 152), halfway along the Jesús–Santa Eulària highway at Roca Llisa. It boasts a nine- and an eighteen-hole course, both positioned between patches of pine woodlands under the island's central hills. You don't have to be a member to play, but it's an expensive course – green fees are €80, and you'll pay extra for a caddy and for renting a golf buggy, though the price does include club rental.

Yoga

Ibiza is fast establishing itself as one of the Mediterranean's key **yoga** destinations, with a choice of centres run by acclaimed instructors. The island itself, with its benign climate and stunning scenery, makes an inspirational base, with many classes performed in the open air in rural surrounds. All prices quoted below exclude flights and transfers.

Yoga centres

D-Lite 3km south of Sant Carles, Ibiza ☎ 628 791 506, ✇ www.d-liteibizayoga.com.

This very upmarket yoga retreat is based in a historic *finca*, with wonderful grounds and a pool, close to Sant Carles. Rooms come with attractive dark-wood furniture and the bathrooms are sleek and contemporary. Daily rates are €250 per person, which includes an organic breakfast and three hours of Ashtanga, Hatha or Iyengar yoga from a professional instructor. Drop-in yoga sessions cost €15 per person. Open year-round.

Ibiza Yoga Benirràs, Ibiza ☎ 020 7419 0999 (UK), ✇ www.ibizayoga.com; April–Nov. Highly popular Ashtanga yoga retreat, situated in a spectacular location a short walk south from one of Ibiza's finest beaches, with seafood restaurants close by for evening meals. Weekly rates are £325–800 per person (depending on the villa and season) for villa accommodation and three hours of tuition per day, breakfast and lunch. Pagodas (£200–375 per person), teepees (£200–350) and a gazebo are also available on the same deal. Yoga day-passes and week-passes are sometimes available to those not staying on-site.

Jivana Ashram 1km inland from Cala Conta, Ibiza ☎ 971 342 494; May–Oct. Small Ashtanga yoga centre run by friendly, experienced German instructors; there's a maximum of eight per class. Accommodation is in comfortable double rooms, but there's no electricity, so it's an early-to-bed kind of place. Superb beaches are only a short walk away. The weekly rate, including full board, is €380; a half-day class costs €24.

Festivals and events

While Ibiza and Formentera cannot claim to host particularly extravagant **festivals**, celebrations form an important part of the social calendar and present the chance for family get-togethers. Every settlement holds an annual *festa* to celebrate the patron saint of the community, with religious services and cultural events in the village square. All of the *festas* listed

below follow a similar pattern, with Ibizan *ball pagès* (folk dancing) and often a display from another region of Spain, plus some live music of the soft rock variety. Bonfires are lit, *torradas* (barbecues) spit and sizzle, traditional sweet snacks like *bunyols* and *orelletes* are prepared, and there's always plenty of alcohol to lubricate proceedings. Some of the bigger events, like the Sant

Bartomeu celebrations in Sant Antoni on August 24 and the *Anar a Maig* in Santa Eulària, involve spectacular fireworks displays.

"*Molts anys i bons*" (many years and good ones) is the customary festival toast.

January
Festa de Sant Antoni Jan 17, Ibiza.
Festa de Santa Agnès de Corona Jan 21, Ibiza.

February/March
Festa de Santa Eulària Feb 12, Ibiza.
Carnaval Towns and villages on both islands live it up during the week before Lent with marches, fancy-dress parades and classical music concerts.

March/April
Semana Santa Holy Week is widely observed, with thousands assembling to watch the religious processions through Dalt Vila and up to the Puig de Missa in Santa Eulària on Good Friday.
Festa de Sant Francesc March 2, Ibiza.
Festa de Sant Josep March 19, Ibiza.
Festa de Sant Vicent April 5, Ibiza.
Festa de Sant Jordi April 23, Ibiza. Traditional fiesta in Sant Jordi, Ibiza, and book-giving throughout the Pitiuses to mark the day.

May
Anar a Maig First Sun in May. Large festival in Santa Eulària with processions of horse-drawn carts, classical music, a flower festival and a big fireworks finale.
Festa de Sant Ferran May 30, Formentera.

June
Nit de Sant Joan June 23. Midsummer night features huge bonfires and effigy-burning in Sant Joan and throughout the Pitiuses.

July
Día de Verge del Carmen July 15–16. The patron saint of seafarers and fishermen is honoured with parades and the blessing of boats, especially in La Savina and Ibiza Town, where the Verge del Carmen statue is removed from the Església Sant Elm by the fishermen of La Marina and placed in a boat, which then leads a flotilla around the harbour in a ceremony to ask her protection at sea for the year ahead.
Festa de Sant Jaume July 25. Widely celebrated throughout Formentera.

August
Santa Maria de las Neus Aug 5. Celebrated with a special mass in Ibiza Town's cathedral.
Festa de Sant Ciriac Aug 8. Small ceremony in Dalt Vila to commemorate the reconquest of 1235, plus a massive watermelon fight in Es Soto below the walls.
Día de Sant Bartomeu Aug 24. Huge harbourside fireworks display, plus concerts and dancing, in Sant Antoni.
Festa de Sant Agustí Aug 28, Ibiza.

September
Festa de Jesús Sept 8, Ibiza.
Festa de Sant Mateu Sept 21, Ibiza.

October
Verge del Pilar Oct 12, La Mola, Formentera.

Water worship

In addition to the religious festivals, water-worshipping ceremonies (*xacotes pageses*) are performed at springs (*fonts*) and wells (*pous*) throughout the Pitiusan countryside, particularly in Ibiza. These festivals are thought to be Carthaginian in origin, and involve much singing and dancing, in order to give thanks for water in islands plagued by droughts. Some better-known ceremonies include:
July 25 Pou d'en Benet, Benimussa, 4km east of Sant Antoni.
Aug 5 Font des Verger, Es Cubells.
First Sun after Aug 5 Pou Roig, near Sant Jordi.
First Sun after Aug 28 Pou des Rafals, Sant Agustí.
Oct 10 Pou de Forada, 5km northeast of Sant Antoni.
First Sun after Oct 15 Font des Xiquet, near Es Cubells.

Festa de Santa Teresa Oct 15, Es
Cubells, Ibiza.
Festa de Sa Creu Oct 24, Sant Rafel,
Ibiza. Locally made ceramics are displayed
and offered for sale.

November
Festa de Sant Carles Nov 4, Ibiza.
Festa de Santa Gertrudis Nov 16, Ibiza.
Includes prize animal exhibits.

December
Wine festival First weekend in Dec, Sant
Mateu, Ibiza. A tremendously sociable
event, with crowds sampling the vintage
from teapot-shaped glass jugs called
porros, and feasting on barbecued
sobrassada and *butifarra* sausages.
Dia de Sant Francesc Dec 5,
Formentera.
Christmas (*Nadal*) Candlelit services
throughout the Pitiuses.
New Year (*Cap d'Any*) Big parties
in nightclubs and Vara de Rey, Ibiza,
traditionally celebrated in Spain by eating
twelve grapes, one on each strike of the
clock at midnight.

Directory

Accommodation Unless otherwise stated,
accommodation listed in the Places
chapters is open all year. The price range
indicates the cost of the cheapest double
room in high season (June–Sept), including
taxes; this price can vary substantially as
costs are generally highest in August, and
cheaper in early June. It's quite possible
to pay €120 for a room in May that costs
€260 in mid-Aug.
Addresses Most street names are in
Catalan, though some Castilian names
survive: Plaça des Parc is Plaza del Parque
on some maps. Common abbreviations
are c/ for Carrer or Calle (street), Ctra
for Carretera (highway). Note that in
Spain, businesses located on main roads
use kilometre markers to indicate their
location; so the restaurant *Can Caus*
adopts the address Ibiza Town–Santa
Gertrudis, km 3.5. This means that the
restaurant is located 3.5km from the
beginning of the road between Ibiza Town
and Santa Gertrudis.
Airlines Air Berlin ☎901 116 402,
✆www.airberlin.com; Air Europa ☎902
401 501, ✆www.air-europa.com; BMIbaby
☎971 395 565, ✆www.bmibaby.com;
easyJet ☎902 299 992, ✆www.easyjet
.com; First Choice Airways ☎971 394 621,
✆www.firstchoice.co.uk/flights; GB Airways
☎902 111 333, ✆www.gbairways.com;
Iberia ☎902 400 500, ✆www.iberia
.com; Monarch ☎800 099 260, ✆www
.flymonarch.com; Spanair ☎902 929 191,
✆www.spanair.es; Thompson ☎914 141
481, ✆www.thompsonfly.com; Vueling
☎902 333 933, ✆www.vueling.com.

Banks and exchange Spain's currency
is the euro (€). Cashpoints (ATMs) are
extremely widespread and accept all the
main credit and debit cards. Banks offer
the best rates for changing travellers'
cheques and foreign currency, though they
have very limited banking hours (generally
Mon–Sat 9am–2pm). Bureaux de change
are found in all the main resorts, often
staying open until midnight, but their
commission rates are higher. Virtually all
restaurants and large stores accept credit
cards, but you'll often need your passport
or driving licence as ID.
Clubs Clubbing in Ibiza is inordinately
expensive: entrance prices average €30–
40 and can cost anything up to €60. It
pays to seek out advance tickets, available
in the hip bars of San An and Ibiza Town,
which typically save you €6–10 (and
include a free drink), or blag a guest pass
if you can. Drinks are outrageously priced
– soft drinks, including bottled water cost
€6–8; a spirit with a mixer anything up
to €15. Note that none of the clubs offer
free tap water to drink. Sometimes there's
a trickle of warm water in the toilets, but
mains water in Ibiza is very saline and
unpleasant to drink.
Consulates UK, Avgda d'Isidor Macabich
45, Ibiza Town ☎971 301 818 (Mon–Fri
9am–3pm). The nearest Irish (☎971 719
244) and US (☎971 725 051) consulates
are in Mallorca.
Drugs First dubbed "ecstasy island" by
The Sun in 1989, drugs are an integral
part of Ibiza's clubbing scene and each
night hundred of deals are done in the

Fly Less – Stay Longer!

Rough Guides believes in the good that travel does, but we are deeply aware of the impact of fuel emissions on climate change. We recommend taking fewer trips and staying for longer. If you can avoid travelling by air, please use an alternative, especially for journeys of under 1000km/600miles. And always offset your travel at ⊛www.roughguides.com/climatechange.

port bars of Ibiza Town, and in San An. Nevertheless, cocaine, ecstasy, heroin, speed, acid, cannabis and ketamine are all illegal in Spain, and the police have been increasing searches outside clubs (in car parks) and elsewhere. Those caught with small amounts (deemed for personal consumption) are often but not necessarily, released with a caution, but in theory you could be looking at a jail term.

Emergency services For the police, fire brigade or an ambulance call ☎112.
Hospital Can Misses, c/de Corona (☎971 397 000), located in the western suburbs of Ibiza Town. The small, new Hospital de Formentera (☎971 321 212) is at Vénda des Brolls, Sant Francesc, and can deal with most injuries and treatments.
Internet All the main towns and resorts have at least one cybercafé; half an hour costs around €1.
Post Allow a week to ten days for mail within the EU, two weeks for the rest of the world. Post offices (*correu*) open between 8.30am and 1.30pm and are found in all the main towns; some souvenir shops also sell stamps.
Telephones You'll find telephone booths in all towns, villages and resorts taking cash or phonecards (which you can buy at tobacconists, newsagents and some petrol stations). Local calls in the ☎971 Balearic area are very cheap, but mobile numbers cost around €0.70 a minute. International

calls can be made from booths (around €2.50 for four minutes) but the most cost-effective way to dial home is by using an international phonecard (available in the same outlets).

UK mobile phones work in the Balearics, though non-triband US-bought handsets may not. If you are planning a long stay, consider buying a Spanish SIM chip (from €12) from a telecom store. To call Ibiza or Formentera from abroad, dial 00 plus the relevant country code (34 in the UK, Ireland and New Zealand; 11 34 in North America; 11 64 in Australia), followed by the nine-digit number.

To call abroad from Ibiza or Formentera, dial 00 followed by the country code (44 for the UK; 353 for Ireland; 1 for the US and Canada; 61 for Australia; 64 for New Zealand) then the area code minus its zero, and then the number.
Time Ibiza and Formentera follow CET (Central European Time), which is one hour ahead of the UK and six hours ahead of US Eastern Standard Time. Spain adopts daylight saving in winter: clocks go back in the last week in October and forward in the last week of March.
Travel agents For flights back to the UK, contact specialists The Foreign Office (☎971 308 620, ⊛www.foreign-office.com) or Ibiza Travel Shop (☎971 803 175, ⊛www.ibizatravelshop.com).

Chronology

Chronology

c.4500 BC ▶ Neolithic pastoralists from the mainland establish settlements in Ibiza near Santa Agnès, bringing their livestock with them.

1850 BC ▶ Family groups raise cattle and farm the Barbària peninsula, Formentera. Ca Na Costa, a megalithic burial chamber is constructed.

650 BC ▶ Phoenicians arrive in Ibiza, building a fishing village at Sa Caleta, before abandoning this settlement for a safer hilltop site (today's Ibiza Town).

500–146 BC ▶ Punic Era. Ibiza becomes a pivotal part of the Carthaginian Empire, with an imposing capital called Ibosim (today's Ibiza Town). The saltpans are developed, silver and lead mined, and Ibiza prospers thanks to the export of a purple dye extracted from a sea snail. Tanit, Punic goddess of love, death and fertility, is closely linked to the island. Formentera is left unsettled.

146 BC ▶ After the defeat of Carthage, Ibiza achieves confederate status in the Roman Empire. A dual Roman-Carthaginian identity evolves, with Punic temples preserved alongside Roman monuments.

70 ▶ Formentera is resettled by the Romans, its inhabitants surviving by farming and fishing, and its population reaching 3000.

74 ▶ Ibosim renamed Ebusus, as the Romans erase Punic identity. Agriculture suffers as olive oil, wine and production falls under the centralized *latifundia* farming system.

100–450 ▶ Agricultural land is slowly abandoned and Ibiza is reduced to being a minor trading post in a fading Roman Empire.

455 ▶ Vandal invaders briefly control the islands.

533–901 ▶ Byzantine forces usurp the Vandals, though they make no attempt to colonize. Ibiza and Formentera are subject to waves of attacks by Normans and Vikings. Gradually the Moors establish influence in the Balearics.

902–1235 ▶ The Moorish Emir of Córdoba conquers the Balearics, ushering in a period of relative prosperity and stability. Irrigation channels are constructed, rice and sugar cane introduced, and the islands are renamed Yebisah and Faramantira.

1235 ▶ Catalan conquest. Self-government brought in, Catalan becomes the official language, the islands are renamed Eivissa and Formentera, and Catholicism is made the official religion.

1348 ▶ Bubonic plague decimates the population in both islands. Formentera is abandoned.

1350–1585 ▶ Moorish and Turkish pirates repeatedly target the Balearics, destroying Santa Eulària in 1545. A network of coastal defence towers and the colossal walls of Dalt Vila are constructed.

1697 ▶ Formentera resettled.

1714 ▸ Castilian replaces Catalan control, leading to less local autonomy. The influence of Catholicism grows; a dozen new parish churches are constructed.

1700s and 1880s ▸ Pirate attacks diminish as Ibizan corsairs challenge Moorish buccaneers.

1871 ▸ Spanish state sells saltpans to a private company to finance its war against Cuban nationalists.

1890s ▸ Introduction of ferry services between Ibiza and the mainland.

1930s ▸ First tourists, mainly artists and writers, visit the islands.

1936–39 ▸ Spanish Civil War. Ibiza and Formentera are bitterly divided along Nationalist and Republican lines. Over a hundred Nationalist prisoners are massacred in Dalt Vila. Concentration camp built in La Savina to house anti-Francoists.

1950s ▸ Bohemian travellers return to the islands, mixing with Spanish leftists and resident artists. A beatnik scene develops in Ibiza Town.

1953 ▸ Thomas Cook includes Ibiza as a tourist destination for the first time. The journey from the UK involves several trains and ferries.

1960s ▸ Hundreds of new hotels constructed in Ibiza and Formentera to serve the burgeoning tourist industry. Sant Antoni is developed into a package resort and thousands of mainlanders move to the island for work. Vietnam draft-dodgers, hippies and "beats" flood to the islands; Pink Floyd record *More* in Formentera.

1965 ▸ Annual tourist arrivals reach 102,000.

1966 ▸ Ibiza airport opens to international flights. Forty-five percent of the population still work in agriculture.

1970s ▸ Beach resorts are constructed across Ibiza. Hippies and police clash over commune evictions and nudity. Actors including Denholm Elliot, Elizabeth Taylor and Laurence Olivier make Santa Eulària a thespian Mecca.

1973 ▸ *Pacha* opens just outside Ibiza Town. Annual tourist numbers reach 500,000.

1976 ▸ *Amnesia* is converted from a farmhouse to a club.

1978 ▸ *Café del Mar* opens in Sant Antoni.

1980s ▸ Wham!'s "Club Tropicana" video is filmed in Ibiza. Acts including Spandau Ballet and Freddie Mercury perform at *Ku*, Europe's greatest club. Ibiza becomes identified with hooliganism as drunken Brits rampage through Sant Antoni.

1987 ▸ Rave pioneers Paul Oakenfold, Danny Rampling and pals visit Ibiza, discover ecstasy and the music of Argentine-born *Amnesia* resident Alfredo, and return to England to kick off the acid-house scene.

1988 ▸ One-time Velvet Underground singer Nico, an Ibizaphile, dies of a brain hemorrhage on the island.

1989 ▶ Ibiza dubbed "ecstasy island" by *The Sun*.

1990-91 ▶ Plans to develop the Salines region for housing and hotels are vigorously opposed by environmentalists; the Balearic government ultimately classifies it as an ANEI (Área Natural de Especial Interés) and the plan is thrown out.

1993 ▶ The first of the *Café del Mar* electronica compilations is released; the series eventually sells 9 million copies.

1995 ▶ Manumission arrives in Ibiza, and quickly takes over the entire *Ku* club.

1998 ▶ British consul Michael Birkett resigns his post, describing the drunken antics of his compatriots as "degenerate".

1999 ▶ Ibiza's first left-wing administration, the Pacte Progressita, is elected, the vote echoing public anger concerning overdevelopment and proposals to build a golf course at Cala d'Hort. Tourist arrivals top 2 million. Ibiza's Dalt Vila, Salines saltpans and Puig des Molins are declared a UNESCO World Heritage Site.

2000 ▶ Superclub era peaks as over a dozen British clubs host nights in Ibiza.

2005-06 ▶ Thousands march against a vast road-building programme of highways, tunnels and underpasses across southern Ibiza, but the work goes on.

2007 ▶ Ibiza returns a leftist administration for only the second time in its history, as public anger against the new highways is reflected in the ballot box.

Language

Spanish

Because virtually everyone can speak it, Spanish has become Ibiza's and Formentera's lingua franca. Until the early 1960s, when there was a mass influx of Castilian Spanish speakers, Eivissenc, the local dialect of Catalan, was the main language in the islands. Eivissenc Catalan was still spoken after the Civil War, despite the efforts of Franco, who banned the language in the media and schools across Catalan-speaking areas of eastern Spain.

However, although Catalan is still the dominant tongue in rural areas and small villages, **Castilian Spanish** is more common in the towns. Only 38 percent of Ibizan residents (the proportion is slightly higher in Formentera) now speak Catalan, a situation the Balearic government is trying to reverse by pushing through a programme of Catalanization. Virtually all street signs are now in Catalan, and it's the main medium of education in schools and colleges.

English-speaking visitors to Ibiza are usually able to get by without any Spanish or Catalan, as **English** is widely understood, especially in the resorts. In Formentera, the situation is slightly different: many people can speak a little English, but as most of their visitors are German and Italian, the islanders tend to learn those languages, and you may have some communication difficulties from time to time. If you want to make an effort, it's probably best to stick to learning Spanish – and maybe try to pick up a few phrases of Catalan. You'll get a good reception if you at least try to communicate in one of these languages.

For more than a brief introduction to Spanish, pick up a copy of the Rough Guide **Spanish Dictionary Phrasebook**.

Pronunciation

The rules of **pronunciation** are straightforward and strictly observed. In Ibiza and Formentera, the lisp-like qualities of mainland Castilian are not common – *cerveza* is usually pronounced "servesa", not "thervetha". Unless there's an accent, words ending in **d**, **l**, **r** and **z** are **stressed** on the last syllable; all others on the second last. All **vowels** are pure and short; combinations have predictable results.

c is soft before e and i, hard otherwise.

g works the same way – a guttural h sound (like the ch in loch) before e or i, and a hard g elsewhere – *gigante* becomes "higante".

h is always silent.

j the same sound as a guttural g: *jamón* is pronounced "hamon".

ll sounds like an English y: *tortilla* is pronounced "torteeya".

n as in English unless it has a tilde (accent) over it, when it becomes ny: *mañana* sounds like "man-yana".

A few Catalan phrases

When pronouncing place names, watch out especially for words with the letter **j** – it's not "Hondal" but "Jondal", as in English. Note also that **x** is almost always a "sh" sound – Xarraca is pronounced "sharrarca". The word for a hill, *puig*, is a tricky one, pronounced "pootch".

If you want to learn more, try *Parla Català* (Pia), a good English–Catalan phrasebook, together with either the Collins or Routledge dictionary. For more serious students, the excellent *Catalan in Three Months* (Stuart Poole, UK), a combined paperback and tape package, is recommended.

Greetings and responses

Hello	Hola	**Do you speak**	Parla
Goodbye	Adéu	**English**	Anglés?
Good morning	Bon dia	**I (don't) speak**	(No) Parlo
Good afternoon	Bona tarda/	**Catalan**	Català
/night	nit	**My name is…**	Em dic…
Yes	Sí	**What's your name?**	Com es diu?
No	No	**I am … English**	Sóc…
OK	Val		…anglès(a)
Please	Per favor	**…Scottish**	…escocès(a)
Thank you	Gràcies	**…Welsh**	…gallès(a)
See you later	Fins després	**…Irish**	…irlandès(a)
Sorry	Ho sento	**…Australian**	…australià/ana
Excuse me	Perdoni	**…from New**	soc neozelandès
How are you?	Com va?	**Zealand**	
I (don't) understand	(No) ho entec	**…Canadian**	…canadenc(a)
Not at all/You're welcome	De res	**…American**	…americà/ana

v sounds a little more like b, *vino* becoming "beano".

x has an s sound before consonants, and a normal x sound before vowels.
z is the same as s.

Basic words and phrases

Basics

Yes, No, OK	Sí, No, Vale
Please, Thank you	Por favor, Grácias
Where?, When?	¿Dónde?, ¿Cuándo?
What?, How much?	¿Qué?, ¿Cuánto?
Here	Aquí
There	Allí, Allá
This, That	Esto, Eso
Now	Ahora
Then	Más tarde
Open, Closed	Abierto/a, Cerrado/a
With, Without	Con, Sin
Good, Bad	Bueno/a, Malo/a
Big, Small	Gran(de), Pequeño/a
Cheap, Expensive	Barato/a, Caro/a
Hot, Cold	Caliente, Frío/a

More, Less	Más, Menos
Today, Tomorrow	Hoy, Mañana
Yesterday	Ayer
The bill	La cuenta

Greetings and responses

Hello, Goodbye	Hola, Adiós
Good morning	Buenos días
Good afternoon/ night	Buenas tardes/ noches
See you later	Hasta luego
Sorry	Lo siento/ discúlpeme
Excuse me	Con permiso/perdón
How are you?	¿Cómo está (usted)?

I (don't) understand	(No) entiendo
Not at all/You're welcome	De nada
Do you speak English?	¿Habla (usted) inglés?
I (don't) speak Spanish	(No) Hablo éspañol
My name is…	Me llamo…
What's your name?	¿Cómo se llama usted?
I am English	Soy inglés(a)
Scottish	escocés(a)
Australian	australiano/a
Canadian	canadiense/a
American	americano/a
Irish	irlandés(a)
Welsh	galés(a)

Hotels and transport

I want	Quiero
I'd like	Quisiera
Do you know…?	¿Sabe…?
I don't know	No sé
There is (is there?)	(¿)Hay(?)
Give me…	Deme…
Do you have…?	¿Tiene…?
…the time	…la hora
…a room	…una habitación
…with two beds/ double bed	…con dos camas/ cama matrimonial
…with shower/bath	…con ducha/baño
for one person	para una persona
for two people	para dos personas
for one night (one week)	para una noche (una semana)
It's fine	Está bien
It's too expensive	Es demasiado caro
Can one…?	¿Se puede…?
camp (near) here?	¿…acampar aqui (cerca)?
It's not very far	No es muy lejos
How do I get to…?	¿Por dónde se va a…?
Left	Izquierda
Right	Derecha
Straight on	Todo recto
Where is…?	¿Dónde está…?
…the bus station	…la estación de autobuses
…the bus stop	…la parada
…the nearest bank	…el banco más cercano
…the post office	…el correo/la oficina de correos
…the toilet	…el baño/ aseo/ servicio

Where does the bus to…leave from?	¿De dónde sale el autobús para…?
I'd like a (return) ticket to…	Quisiera un billete (de ida y vuelta) para…
What time does it leave?	¿A qué hora sale ?
(arrive in…)?	(llega a…)?
What is there to eat?	¿Qué hay para comer?

Days of the week

Monday	lunes
Tuesday	martes
Wednesday	miércoles
Thursday	jueves
Friday	viernes
Saturday	sábado
Sunday	domingo

Numbers

1	un/uno/una
2	dos
3	tres
4	cuatro
5	cinco
6	seis
7	siete
8	ocho
9	nueve
10	diez
11	once
12	doce
13	trece
14	catorce
15	quince
16	dieciséis
17	diecisiete
18	dieciocho
19	diecinueve
20	veinte
21	vientiuno
30	treinta
40	cuarenta
50	cincuenta
60	sesenta
70	setenta
80	ochenta
90	noventa
100	cien(to)
200	doscientos
500	quinientos
1000	mil
2000	dos mil

LANGUAGE

Basic words and phrases

Food and drink

aceitunas	olives
agua	water
ahumados	smoked fish
alioli	garlic mayonnaise
al ajillo	with olive oil and garlic
a la marinera	seafood cooked with garlic, onions and white wine
a la parilla	charcoal-grilled
a la plancha	grilled on a hot plate
a la romana	fried in batter
albóndigas	meatballs
almejas	clams
anchoas	anchovies
arroz	rice
asado	roast
bacalao	cod
berenjena	aubergine/eggplant
bocadillo	bread-roll sandwich
boquerones	small, anchovy-like fish, usually served in vinegar
café (con leche)	(white) coffee
calamares	squid
cangrejo	crab
cebolla	onion
cerveza	beer
champiñones	mushrooms
chorizo	spicy sausage
croquetas	croquettes, usually with bits of ham in them
cuchara	spoon
cuchillo	knife
dorada	gilt head
empanada	slices of fish/meat pie
ensalada	salad
ensaladilla	Russian salad (diced vegetables in mayonnaise, often with tuna)
fresa	strawberry
gambas	prawns
Hierbas	sweet Ibizan liqueur
hígado	liver
huevos	eggs

jamón serrano	cured ham
jamón de york	regular ham
langostinos	langoustines
lechuga	lettuce
manzana	apple
mejillones	mussels
mero	grouper
mojo	garlic dressing available in rojo (spicy "red" version) and verde ("green, made with coriander)
naranja	orange
ostras	oysters
pan	bread
patatas alioli	potatoes in garlic mayonnaise
patatas bravas	fried potatoes in a spicy tomato sauce
pimientos	peppers
pimientos de padrón	small peppers, with the odd hot one
piña	pineapple
pisto	assortment of cooked vegetables, similar to ratatouille
plátano	banana
pollo	chicken
pulpo	octopus
queso	cheese
raor	wrasse
(Sa) Caleta café	coffee made with brandy and orange peel
salchicha	sausage
setas	oyster mushrooms
sobrasada	sausage
sopa	soup
té	tea
tenedor	fork
tomate	tomato
tortilla española	potato omelette
tortilla francesa	plain omelette
vino (blanco/ rosado/tinto)	(white/rosé/red) wine
zarzuela	fish stew
zumo	juice

Glossary

ajuntament town hall

avinguda (avgda) avenue

Baal main Carthaginian deity, "the rider of the clouds", associated with the cult of child sacrifice

baluard bastion

barrio suburb or neighbourhood

cala cove

cami road

campo countryside

can, c'an, cas or c'as house

capella chapel

carrer (c/) street

carretera highway

casament Ibizan farmhouse

castell castle

chiringuito beach café-bar, which usually serves snacks

chupito shot of liquor

churrigueresque fancifully ornate form of Baroque art, named after its leading exponents, the Spaniard José Churriguera (1650–1723) and his extended family

correu post office

cova cave

Ebusus Roman name for Ibiza Town

Ecotax Balearic environmental tax; abandoned in 2004

Eivissa Catalan name for Ibiza, and Ibiza Town

Eivissenc Catalan dialect spoken in the Pitiuses; it's known as "Ibicenco" in Castilian Spanish.

església church

far lighthouse

finca farmhouse

Ibosim Carthaginian name for Ibiza Town

illa island

kiosko beach bar or café

mercat market

mirador lookout

museu museum

parada bus stop

parc park

passeig avenue

plaça square

Pitiuses Southern Balearics: Ibiza, Formentera, Espalmador, Espardell, Tagomago and Conillera are the main islands.

platja beach

pou well

puig hill

punta point

riu river

salines saltpans

serra mountain

torre tower

torrent seasonal stream, dried-up river bed

urbanización housing estate

Yebisah Arabic name for Ibiza

Available from all good bookstores D: Rough Guide DIRECTIONS

For more information go to www.roughguides.com

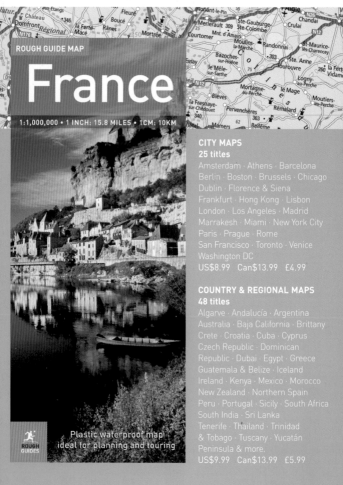

Visit us online
www.roughguides.com

Information on over 25,000 destinations around the world

- **Read** Rough Guides' trusted travel info

- **Access** exclusive articles from Rough Guides authors

- **Update** yourself on new books, maps, CDs and other products

- **Enter** our competitions and win travel prizes

- **Share** ideas, journals, photos & travel advice with other users

- **Earn** points every time you contribute to the Rough Guide
  community and get rewards

BROADEN YOUR HORIZONS

Listen Up!

"You may be used to the Rough Guide series being comprehensive, but nothing will prepare you for the exhaustive Rough Guide to World Music . . . one of our books of the year."

Sunday Times, London

Rough Guide Music Titles

The Beatles • Blues • Bob Dylan • Classical Music
Elvis • Frank Sinatra • Heavy Metal • Hip-Hop
iPods, iTunes & music online • Jazz • Book of Playlists
Led Zeppelin • Opera • Pink Floyd • Punk • Reggae
Rock • The Rolling Stones • Soul and R&B • World
Music Vol 1 & 2 • Velvet Underground

Visit the real Ibiza

Can Pere is a rural hotel offering stylish accommodation, a fine restaurant and a tranquil location just 8km from Ibiza Town

**www.canperehotel.com
(0034) 971 196 000**

small print & **Index**

SMALL PRINT

A Rough Guide to Rough Guides

In 1981, Mark Ellingham, a recent graduate in English from Bristol University, was travelling in Greece on a tiny budget and couldn't find the right guidebook. With a group of friends he wrote his own guide, combining a contemporary, journalistic style with a practical approach to travellers' needs. That first Rough Guide was a student scheme that became a publishing phenomenon. Today, Rough Guides include recommendations from shoestring to luxury and cover hundreds of destinations around the globe, including almost every country in the Americas and Europe, more than half of Africa and most of Asia and Australasia. Millions of readers relish Rough Guides' wit and inquisitiveness as much as their enthusiastic, critical approach and value-for-money ethos. The guides' ever-growing team of authors and photographers is spread all over the world.

In the early 1990s, Rough Guides branched out of travel, with the publication of Rough Guides to World Music, Classical Music and the Internet. All three have become benchmark titles in their fields, spearheading the publication of a range of more than 350 titles under the Rough Guide name, including phrasebooks, waterproof maps, music guides from Opera to Heavy Metal, reference works as diverse as Conspiracy Theories and Shakespeare, and popular culture books from iPods to Poker. Rough Guides also produce a series of more than 120 World Music CDs in partnership with World Music Network.

Visit www.roughguides.com to see our latest publications.

Rough Guide travel images are available for commercial licensing at www.roughguidespictures.com

Publishing information

This second edition published April 2008 by Rough Guides Ltd, 80 Strand, London WC2R 0RL. 345 Hudson St, 4th Floor, New York, NY 10014, USA.

Distributed by the Penguin Group
Penguin Books Ltd, 80 Strand, London WC2R 0RL
Penguin Group (USA), 375 Hudson Street, NY 10014, USA
14 Local Shopping Centre, Panchsheel Park, New Delhi 110017, India
Penguin Group (Australia), 250 Camberwell Road, Camberwell, Victoria 3124, Australia
Penguin Group (Canada), 10 Alcorn Avenue, Toronto, ON M4V 1E4, Canada
Penguin Group (NZ), 67 Apollo Drive, Mairangi Bay, Auckland 1310, New Zealand
Typeset in Bembo and Helvetica to an original design by Henry Iles.

Cover concept by Peter Dyer.

Printed and bound in China
© Iain Stewart 2008

No part of this book may be reproduced in any form without permission from the publisher except for the quotation of brief passages in reviews.
208pp includes index

A catalogue record for this book is available from the British Library
ISBN 978-1-85828-349-4

The publishers and authors have done their best to ensure the accuracy and currency of all the information in Ibiza DIRECTIONS, however, they can accept no responsibility for any loss, injury, or inconvenience sustained by any traveller as a result of information or advice contained in the guide.

1   3   5   7   9   8   6   4   2

Help us update

We've gone to a lot of effort to ensure that the second edition of Ibiza DIRECTIONS is accurate and up-to-date. However, things change – places get "discovered", opening hours are notoriously fickle, restaurants and rooms raise prices or lower standards. If you feel we've got it wrong or left something out, we'd like to know, and if you can remember the address, the price, the phone number, so much the better.

Please send your comments with the subject line "Ibiza DIRECTIONS Update" to ✉mail@roughguides.com. We'll credit all contributions and send a copy of the next edition (or any other Rough Guide if you prefer) for the very best emails.

Have your questions answered and tell others about your trip at ⓦcommunity.roughguides.com

Rough Guide credits

Text editor: James Smart
Layout: Anita Singh
Photography: Lydia Evans, Demetrio Carrasco
Cartography: Jasbir Sandhu
Picture editor: Harriet Mills
Proofreader: Anne Burgot
Production: Rebecca Short
Cover design: Chloë Roberts

The author

Author of the *Rough Guide to Guatemala* and contributor to the Rough Guides to Central America and Spain, Iain Stewart first took his bucket and spade to the Balearics as a toddler and has been returning regularly ever since. He lives in Brighton.

Acknowledgements

Thanks to my editor James Smart for his expertise and excellent suggestions, and to all the Rough Guides team. In Ibiza, Enrique Moreno was the perfect host as ever, and Martin Davies a font of knowledge. It's always great to catch up with my Ibiza-based pals Andy and Chrissie, Johnny and Cid, Hannah, Shirell and Nir, Jill, the Charltons and Jasmine. And, as ever, it's great to enjoy the island with my extended family: darling Fee, Louis Yoshi and Monty Kenji, Susan and Aubs, Betty, Jan, Dave and Simone.

Readers' letters

Thanks to all those readers who wrote in with suggestions and updates (and apologies if we've inadvertently omitted or misspelt anybody's name): Roger Dubois; W. G. McDougal; Sara Parle; Roger Pebody; John Redston; Carol Saunders; Lorna A. Wilson; Caroline Wright.

Photo credits

All images © Rough Guides except the following:

Front cover picture: Cala Salada Beach © Ripani Massimo/4cornersimages
Back cover picture: Girl dancing, Es vive Hotel © Alamy
p.10 Salines saltpans © DK Images
p.12 Can Talaias © Iain Stewart
p.13 Finca Can Xuxu © Iain Stewart
p.14 Carl Cox at Space © Space
p.15 Pacha © Pacha
p.15 Privilege © Privilege
p.16 Pedalos on beach © Iain Stewart
p.18 Sunset on beach at Café Mambo © Debbie Bragg/Everynight Images/Alamy
p.19 Cala Salada © Iain Stewart
p.28 La Casita Verde © Chris Dews/Casita Verde
p.36 Carrer de la Verge, Ibiza Town © Jon Arnold Images/Alamy
p.38 Yoga, Ibiza © Visual & Written SL/Alamy
p.40 Torre de ses Portes © Iain Stewart
p.41 Atlantis © Iain Stewart
p.47 Scuba diver with cuttlefish, Ibiza © Wolfgang Polzer/Alamy
p.66 El Hotel © El Hotel
p.77 Pacha © Pacha
p.88 Agroturisme Xarc © Agroturisme Xarc
p.147 Space © Space

Index

Maps are marked in colour

INDEX

INDEX

Ibiza
& Formentera

DIRECTIONS

WRITTEN AND RESEARCHED BY

Iain Stewart

ROUGH
GUIDES

NEW YORK • LONDON • DELHI
www.roughguides.com